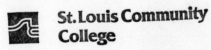

Kitchen Management
For Institutions

Kitchen Management For Institutions

*Economies in Purchasing,
Portioning, and Preparation*

WILLIAM K. DEUEL

Written for
Frank, Fritz, and Suzy

Library of Congress Cataloging in Publication Data

Deuel, William K
    Kitchen management for institutions.

    1. Food service management.   2. Cookery for
institutions, etc.   I. Title.
TX943.D48   642'.5   75-19256
ISBN 0-8104-9462-0

Printed in the United States of America

1	2	3	4	5	6	7	8	9	PRINTING
75	76	77	78	79	80	81	82	83	YEAR

Preface

In talking with others in the business of feeding people, I have heard at all levels the complaint that there was no place to turn for information on most subjects unique to the food industry. General business principles provide surface guidance, but they cannot be used to solve the day-to-day problems confronting the professional kitchen manager; nor can they provide a basis for long-range concerns such as portion control, buying, equipment, menu, pricing, cooking methods—and profit!

This book, based on numerous discussions with others in our business, as well as my own long involvement, addresses itself to these specific problems and concerns. It is meant to be a sound, practical tool—a handbook rather than a treatise, a compendium rather than a thesis.

The book is divided into two major sections. The first deals with those operational controls, systems, and principles, without which any feeding institution is a haphazard enterprise at best. The second section covers food preparation, including methods, economies, and recipes.

Certainly the success or failure of any feeding business does not hinge on one's willingness to follow the principles and methods espoused in a single book. It is my hopeful assumption, however, that those using this work will find it a genuine aid in adapting to problems and opportunities as they occur.

The book underscores economical methods for preparing nutritious, high quality foods; the entire system, administrative and functional, is based on low-budget cookery. The convenience and additional profits of low-budget menus make this volume a worthwhile resource for restaurants and food service institutions of all types.

WILLIAM K. DEUEL

Venice, California

Contents

Part Two

Kitchen Management
For Institutions

Part One

—————

Part One presents information regarding the administrative functions of food producing units. These include a method of establishing uniform areas of food production through adopting standard patterns for the type of foods to be used; an in-depth analysis of portion control as it will apply to varying types of operations; purchasing procedures and suggestions for adapting the buying operation to the portion and production program; as well as information pertaining to personnel and basic equipment needs.

The ideas in this section are flexible; they apply to convenience feeding operations of almost every size. But because there is very little available information dealing with operations of modest size—those restaurants with a daily volume of three hundred to nine hundred dollars and/or institutions feeding between 100 to 350 people per meal—the discussions have been confined essentially to this general category.

1.

Establishing a System of Food Operation

Subsistence foods are those prepared in volume to feed a predetermined number of people. They are, as the name implies, the basic foods needed for daily survival. Volume feeding involves adopting a recipe to produce an exact number of portions to fit a given situation. While restaurants, where food is ordered from a menu, will have need for several such preparations, institutional feeding operations normally offer either no selection or a very limited choice. Hospitals, homes for the aged, convalescent organizations, school cafeterias, or detention organizations have less need for daily variety and more need for volume with fixed recipes and methods of operation.

For any low-budget volume-feeding operation the need is to create a uniform system of food preparation. Once an acceptable recipe has been decided upon for continuing use, it must be formalized as to exact ingredients, grade, and quantities to yield a predetermined number of portions. By creating a library of food preparation formulas for each recipe, each designed to fit the needs of a particular restaurant or institution, an entire system of controls begins to emerge. Once a number of such annotated recipes is accumulated, a routine schedule of food preparation can be established. As the preparation staff becomes familiar with each formula, mistakes are minimized and productivity increases markedly.

Variety, both in basic foods and methods of preparation should not be eliminated. Particularly if one's audience is captive, as is often the case in an institution, variety is essential. Thus, selecting or creating formulas to fit a particular situation requires judgment and taste.

The restaurant will have the wider latitude because the emphasis can be on taste and appearance, with nutritional values left for the consumer to decide upon. Institutions of all kinds will find their needs more confining and demanding, for they must stress nutrition as well as taste, texture, and visual appearance. Larger institutions do, of course, have dietitians, who can make suggestions for enrichments to ordinary food formulas to maintain acceptable nutritional standards. (Usually food enrichments will not substantially affect predetermined costs, since most added food values, such as dry milk solids, wheat germ, soy flour, or enriched white flour, are inexpensive.)

Once a specific recipe has been arranged and cost projections made, one will find that other foods prepared in a similar manner won't vary much in cost from the original. This makes cost figuring and adjustment of additional recipes less tedious. The production formula for a 6-ounce serving of browned beef stew, for instance, will have almost the same per portion cost as: braised lamb with vegetables; veal fricassee with vegetables; creamed chicken with vegetables; and braised short-ribs of beef with vegetables. In each instance the amount of meat and extenders in each portion will be equal in weight.

Cost projections must be accurate to make a formula valid and reliable, yet the formula should be set up to allow for cost fluctuations. Such fluctuations, when figured within the context of a formula, are usually miniscule. For example, if the meat in a formula increases in cost by 10 percent after the projection has been designed to yield 100 portions with a total meat cost of $30.00 or $.30 per portion. Such a substantial increase, when reduced to the cost of each serving unit produced, raises the actual cost of a portion by only $.03. This increase can be eliminated by very slightly reducing the usual meat contents of the recipe, or by slightly increasing the other extenders in order to produce additional portions, or by slightly reducing the weight or size of the portion to be served. None of these steps would materially affect the quality or the quantity of the food.

A preliminary cost analysis can be quickly arrived at by determining the approximate cost for the total ingredients and then the estimated number of portions the mass is expected to yield can be priced in the unit fashion. If the portion yield fits roughly within the cost allowances needed, a more accurate cost analysis can be made by either requesting bids from purveyors or by trial-and-error—producing the formula in the kitchen and keeping an accurate cost breakdown. Ingredients can be adjusted up or down to stay within reasonable costs while producing a quality product. In such cases always serve the maximum amount of food possible within or at the cost allowance. If the end product is below the portion cost allowance set up as a standard, the product should be carefully surveyed to assure that the house quality standards are maintained or exceeded. No formula should be used which will not meet the highest standards in taste, texture, and visual appeal.

The advantages of a standardized, custom designed series of formulas can be summed up as follows:

1. Recipes best suited to the operation are always available and production-ready.
2. The system creates a uniform method of procedure requiring decreased supervision as the kitchen personnel become familiar with each recipe.
3. Recipes can be specifically adapted to fit the work qualifications of the kitchen personnel.
4. Cooking procedures can be those best suited to the kitchen equipment of the establishment.
5. Ingredients can be selected for their taste and texture in the end-product (especially meats which will suffer the least shrinkage in the cooking process).
6. Formulas can be used as buying guides.
7. Fixed cost projections lighten supervisory tasks, leaving only the mechanics of portioning as a supervisory area.

In converting a functioning operation to low-budget cookery or in adapting low-budget cookery to a new organization, details are many and important. One of the more important considerations, portion control, is discussed next.

2.

Establishing a
Portion Control System

The portioning program best suited to the commercial restaurant can be used as a model for other types of feeding organizations. In the restaurant if the portion is penurious the establishment will lose customers; if it becomes too generous the house will lose money. The perfection of portioning is a system which strikes a balance between a satisfied customer and a profitable operation.

Another reason for first turning to the commercial restaurant for a foundation from which to build other systems is its long history of dealing with the portioning problem. Almost from its inception the commercial establishment has had to establish certain rules of operation regarding how much could be given a customer in exchange for his money.

The following examples have long-standing validity for the commercial restaurant and may be used to establish and maintain reasonable proportions.

Arriving at Portion Sizes

To create a portion system tailored to fit a given establishment, examples of how differences in amounts and costs will vary according to service will best illustrate a method of creating a cost control system and a portion system in one operation.

If liver is purchased at $.98 a pound, or $.06 an ounce, a 3-ounce (normal) portion will cost $.18. If the liver is then served with 2 strips of bacon which has been cut with 26 slices to the pound and had a cost of $.78 per pound or $.03 per strip, the portion cost will rise to $.24. If 4 ounces of liver are served with 3 strips of bacon the portion cost will be $.33. An alternative would be to serve the liver with fried onions, which have a cost of $.04 for 3 ounces. Since the amount of onions would be the same on either service, the first 3-ounce portion would have a total cost of $.22 and the 4-ounce portion a cost of $.28. If the liver is purchased whole and fabricated in the kitchen and an average of 2% unusable trim results, the cost per portion should be adjusted upward by $.02 to cover the loss.

A broad-breasted turkey with a raw cost of $.40 per pound will yield cooked meat at the rate of $1.20 per pound, or three times the cost of the raw price for the whole bird. This rule applies to all sizes of birds prepared for institutional use and cooked under the slow roasting process described in the second section of this book. High heat cooking will diminish the portionable meat by approximately 20 percent.

If the meat is removed from the carcass and preportioned into uniform 3-ounce amounts at a cost of $0.0750 per ounce, the portion cost for the meat will be $0.2250, to which will have to be added the cost of the dressing and gravy, resulting in a total portion cost of approximately $.30. If a 4-ounce portion of meat is served, the cost per portion will rise only by the cost of the meat, or $0.0750, since the dressing and gravy costs will remain the same. If in the process of fabrication the kitchen produces only 20 portions from a bird which should have had a yield of 28 portions, the meat cost will jump to $.09 per ounce. Thus, a 3-ounce portion will cost $.27 instead of $0.2250.

Dinner 1

Meal Courses	Ounces
Appetizer	2
Soup	5
Salad	4
Entree	5
Vegetable	3
Potatoes	4
Bread	3
Dessert	3
Beverage	7
Total	36

To arrive at the amount of food to be served, the quantity of what the customer will require at a specific time should be taken into careful consideration. Under average circumstances the typical customer will consume no more than 1½ pounds of food at the prime meal of the day. This includes leaders, dessert, and beverage. To serve more than this total will result in waste. The two breakdowns of complete dinners, demonstrate both wastefully excessive and reasonable portioning.

Since the guest will require no more than 24 ounces of food, this would result in the service of more food than is either required or will be consumed. Furthermore, the house will be creating a 30 percent overage in its food costs for such a service.

Correct portioning would result in reduced amounts of food and/or the elimination of certain leaders—soup, salad, or appetizer—thus cutting the dinner down to more modest and realistic proportions. Proper portion controls would yield this service:

Dinner 2

Meal courses	Ounces
Appetizer, soup, or salad	3
Entree	4
Vegetable and/or potato	5
Bread	3
Beverage	7
Total	22

By ascertaining how much food is to be served per meal, costs are kept under control and the patron is given a more balanced meal. Dinner 2 makes dessert an option left for the customer to decide. He has already been served a nutritious, well-balanced dinner and may not wish to extend it.

In arriving at reasonable portions for sandwiches and snacks, consider that the customer is indicating a relatively light desire for food. If he wanted bulk he would probably order something else. In determining portions for sandwiches and snacks, keep in mind that the typical guest will also order a beverage, which will add to the overall bulk of the serving. Tables 1 and 5 offer suggested portion quantities for both sandwiches and snacks.

Portioning Bulk Cooked Foods

In portioning of cooked foods which combine meat, sauce, and vegetables, extenders form the bulk of the food. In braises of all kinds where all the ingredients are combined, the formula for service will be 1/3 meat and 2/3 extender, which includes the sauce. For maximum control such foods should be served in casseroles or baking dishes of established sizes. If potatoes are included in the bulk extenders and the service is as a single dish entree (with the possible addition of bread and butter) the luncheon service should be 8 ounces and the dinner service 10 ounces. When potatoes are served separately, luncheon should be 6 ounces and dinner 8 ounces.

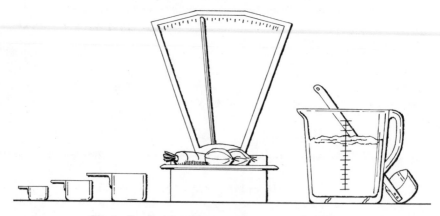

Fig. 1. *Food scale with measuring cups and a ladle.*

For meats braised separately, such as pot roast served on a bed of noodles, or with vegetables or steamed rice, 3 ounces of cooked meat and 4 ounces of other ingredients is considered standard. Braised Swiss steak or cutlets of any kind cooked by moist heat should weigh 3 ounces per service on a bed of rice or noodles or 4 ounces if served only with a sauce or gravy.

Meat loaf service is measured rather than weighed. If the loaves are cooked in pans 3 inches deep and 4 inches wide, a half-inch thick slice with 2 ounces of sauce or gravy constitutes a standard serving. The same portion will prevail if the meat loaf is served on a bed of other foods such as noodles. Meatballs with approximately the same ingredients as meat loaf call for 4 ounces of meat (or sufficient balls to make that amount). This service is the same for either spaghetti and meat balls or noodles and meat balls.

For such dishes as chili and macaroni, chili and spaghetti, Spanish macaroni, or meat sauce with any pastas, the service will be 2 ounces

Fig. 2. *Plates and casserole showing portioning of cooked food.*

of meat in sauce to 6 ounces of cooked pasta products. For similar cheese dishes such as macaroni and cheese, the same ratio holds—2 ounces of cheese to 6 ounces of pasta and sauce. Usually in such dishes the cheese will be used as a topping with the flavor injected by using a

Table 1.
Suggested Portions for Appetizers

Item	*Portion*
Fruit Juice	3 ounces
	32 to No. 10 can
	15 to No. 5 can
	6 to No. 2 can
Fruit cup	3 ounces—24 to No. 10 can
Clam cocktail,	
Cherrystone	3
Littleneck	4
Crabmeat cocktail, cooked, or canned meat	1 ½ ounces
Shrimp cocktail,	
cooked cocktail size	2 ounces
under 16 to the pound, fresh	3 pieces
Oyster cocktail, New Jersey counts	3 pieces
Thin vegetable and meat base soup	7 ounces
Bisque or creamed soup	5 ounces
Consommé	5 ounces

well seasoned sauce. This will make portioning more accurate since if the cheese is combined and stirred into the other ingredients it will be difficult to have a uniform amount in each dish. Straight chili con carne should be served in 6 ounce bowls (or 8 ounces if beans are included). The meat proportion of a recipe should be 2 ounces per service, with sauce making up the bulk.

Table 2.
Meat Portion Sizes and Amounts
to Purchase for 100 Portions

Cut	Preparation	Cooked Portion Size (ounces)	Estimated Bulk Purchase (pounds)
Beef			
Rib	7-rib standing roast	2½	44
		3	50
		4	66
		5	86
		6	100
		8	135
Round	Chicken fried steaks, Swiss steaks, roasts	2	40
		3	55
		4	75
		5	90
		6	110
Sirloin butts (boneless)	Steaks, quality roasts	3	32
		4	50
		5	62
		6	75
Ground beef	Meat loaf (all meat)	3	35
		4	45
		5	58
		6	70
Ground beef	For extended meat loaves containing cereals or vegetables	3	20
		4	26
		5	35
		6	42

Table 2.
Meat Portion Sizes and Amounts
to Purchase for 100 Portions *(Continued)*

Cut	Preparation	Cooked Portion Size (ounces)	Estimated Bulk Purchase (pounds)
Lamb			
Leg, bone-in	Roast	2½	37
		3	45
		4	60
Shoulder, boneless	Stews, braises or rolled roast	3	35
		4	45
Veal			
Leg, bone-in	Roast	2½	35
		3	38
		4	50
Shoulder, boneless	Roast, stews or fricassees	2½	25
		3	30
		4	41
Pork			
Loin, boneless	Roast	2½	35
		3	47
		4	60
		5	78

Table 3.
Suggested Portions for Popular Entrees

Item	Portion Combination
Meat balls and spaghetti	2 ounces meat 4 ounces spaghetti 3 ounces sauce
Creamed chipped beef	1 ounce meat 4 ounces sauce 2 ounces toast (1 slice and 2 tips)

Table 3.
Suggested Portions for Popular Entrees *(Continued)*

Item	*Portion Combination*
Goulash and dumpling	2 ounces meat 4 ounces sauce 2 ounces dumplings
Browned beef stew and noodles	2 ounces meat 3 ounces sauce 4 ounces noodles
Corned or roast beef hash	2 ounces meat 2 ounces stock 5 ounces potato and onion filler
Ham and lima beans	2 ounces meat 4 ounces beans 2 ounces sauce
Veal stew and noodles	2 ounces meat 5 ounces noodles 2 ounces sauce
Macaroni and cheese	2 ounces cheese 4 ounces macaroni 3 ounces sauce
Beef, chicken, or veal pot pies	2 ounces meat 3 ounces vegetables 3 ounces sauce 2 ounces biscuit dough topping
Veal curry and rice	2 ounces meat 3 ounces sauce 4 ounces steamed rice
Veal cutlet with spanish sauce	3 ounces meat 3 ounces sauce
Pork cutlet and cream gravy	3 ounces meat 3 ounces gravy or sauce

Table 4.
Suggested Portions for Raw Meats

Portion Size

Beef

Boneless beef, boiled	6½ ounces
Swiss steaks	5 ounces
Cube steaks	3-4 ounces
Chicken fried steaks	4-5 ounces
Laminated chipped steaks	3 ounces
Sirloin steaks	8-12 ounces
Minute steaks	6-8 ounces
Hamburger patties	3 ounces
Hamburger steaks	5-7 ounces

Lamb

Rib chops	2 chops, 4 ounces each
Loin chops, thick w/kidney	8 ounces
Loin chops, thin	2 chops, 3 ounces each
Leg steak, boneless	6 ounces

Pork

Tenderloin steaks, breaded	4 ounces
Sausage patties	3 ounces
Chops, bone-in, rib	2 chops, 3 ounces each
Chops, loin	1 thick chop, 6 ounces
Ham steak	6 ounces

Veal

Cutlet, breaded	4 ounces
Liver (calf)	3 ounces
Chop, loin	1 chop, 5 ounces
Chop, rib	1 chop, 6 ounces

Chicken

Broiled	half of 2 pound bird
Fried	half of 2½ pound bird

Other Poultry

Guinea hen	4 portions to a 2½ pound bird
Duck, roast	4 portions to a 4½ pound bird
Turkey	1½ portions to a raw pound
Capon, roast	1¼ portions to a raw pound

Table 4.
Suggested Portions for Raw Meats *(Continued)*

Seafoods   *Portion Size*

Fish fillets (boneless strips)	4 ounces
Trout, boneless	2 portions to a raw pound
Clams, steamed	8 medium size
Oysters, breaded	6 each
Scallops	8 small (or large cut into pieces)
Shrimp, breaded, fried	3 pieces (under 12 to a pound)
Lobster tails, broiled	1 piece, 6 ounces
Fish steaks (various)	8 ounces

Table 5.
Suggested Portions for Various Sandwiches

Item   *Portions for Fillings*

Cold Sandwiches

Beef, cold roast	2 ounces
Beef, corned	2 ounces
Cheese	2 ounces
Chicken, sliced	1½ ounces
Chicken salad	2½ ounces
Ham, cold baked	2 ounces
Lettuce and tomato	4 slices tomato
Sardines	3 pieces or 2 ounces
Tongue, sliced	2 ounces
Tuna salad	2½ ounces
Turkey, cold sliced	1½ ounces

Hot Sandwiches

Bacon and egg	1 egg, 2 slices bacon (1 ounce)
Bacon and tomato	3 slices tomato, 2 slices bacon
Beef, hot roast	2 ounces meat, 3 ounces gravy
Ham and egg	1 egg, 1 ounce ham
Hamburger	3 ounce pattie
Pastrami, hot	3 ounces meat
Pork, hot roast	2 ounces meat, 3 ounces gravy
Turkey, hot	1½ ounces meat, 3 ounces gravy

Table 6.
Suggested Portions for Vegetables

Item	*Fresh**	*Canned*
Asparagus	4 stalks	2 ounces (12 portions No. 2½ can)
Beans, green lima	2 ounces	2 ounces
Beens, green string	2 ounces	2 ounces
Beets	3 portions to pound	3 ounces, sliced or diced
Broccoli	2½ ounces (fresh or frozen)	
Brussels sprouts	2½ ounces (fresh or frozen)	
Cabbage	3 portions to pound	
Carrots	3 ounces	3 ounces
Cauliflower	2½ ounces	
Corn, whole kernel	2 ounces	2 ounces
Eggplant	3 ounces	
Peas, green	2 ounces	2 ounces
Spinach	2 ounces	2 ounces
Tomatoes	2 ounces	3 ounces
Turnips	3 ounces	

*In most cases vegetables will be portioned the same as fresh.

3.

Institutional Portioning

Institutional portioning and food control boils down to reaching a fixed allowable cost for purchase, preparation, and dispensing—and to stay within that cost. To be sure, it is often less simple than it sounds; yet the complexities involved in mass feeding can be reduced to manageable dimensions by adhering scrupulously to sensible portion controls. The Los Angeles County Sheriff's Department, which is responsible for one of the largest systems of institutional feeding in the nation, offers an outstanding example of a highly precise, yet flexible, system of controls. The department's hundreds of feeding units each operate individually yet with such accurate controls that units feeding only 25 persons will serve the same portions at the same cost as units serving 1,000. Making the controls functional was absolutely necessary since the staffs concerned with administration and production vary as much as do the units' modes of operation.

Through adroit structuring of menu offerings and portion controls, the department was able to maintain in the fiscal year 1973-1974 an actual food cost of $0.3945 per meal for food that when purchased from outside sources in emergencies cost $1.50. This figure covers food as well as civilian labor and each feeding unit must stay within the cost figure prescribed. The kinds and amounts of food to be served for each of the three meals served daily are predetermined at administrative level. Furthermore, this system does not allow for variations in quantity or quality. Feeding program costs are equal for both civilian employees, officers, and executives, as well as inmates in women's and men's detention units and various hospital units.

Although all meats, vegetables, dairy products, and baked goods are produced in one of the units, the Wayside Honor Farm, food costs are figured on a wholesale purchase price basis to cover operating expenses. Thus, each unit, whether jail, hospital, officers' or executives' dining room, portions and dispenses food with a labor and food cost of $2.51 per meal. In every unit the food is prepared by the same production formula and served in the same portioned quantity.

To make such systems functional, each unit must produce foods to coordinated standard formulas. Each weekly series of formulas must be adhered to so that exact quantities of ingredients can be dispatched from the central supply source. Thus, actual control is exerted by the commissary, which supplies only the needed basic ingredients for a specified number of portions. Various units in such a program may produce their own menus, since each series of formulas will be adjusted to fit the cost allowance standards for an entire organization. By making a series of formulas available to any unit, meals may be made diverse and attractive.

For such operations each formula must be adaptable to various quantities. To receive sufficient supplies all that should be required of the production kitchen for their preparation would be an indication of the series to be used and the number of people to be fed. Thus, by adding to or subtracting from the standard formula to arrive at the number of portions to be prepared, the production kitchen can create its own daily recipe. Precision is a necessity, although each formula can allow for a normal amount of over- or underproduction with supplies furnished accordingly. Small fluctuations in numbers of portions produced should be figured into cost projections when the formulas are established.

Tables 7 and 8 offer examples of portioning and production controls used by the Los Angeles County Sheriff's Department. They are self explanatory and are noteworthy for their simplicity. By keeping field functions on a low-key level, personnel problems are reduced to a minimum, making the program functional for small units where personnel capabilities will probably be minimal.

It is possible to design a similar program applicable to individual units not large enough to have the advantage of a commissary supply situation. By coordinating a series of established recipes with a purchasing program, Rest Haven Corporation, a firm which sells franchise convalescent home operations, is able to supply its members with a coordinated food control system designed for use at varying levels. Although not concerned with the cost of the foods produced, their system provides food production recipes with accompanying charts to indicate the amount of ingredients needed for producing portions in a scale of from 10 to 100 units, progressing in units of ten. Each recipe is adaptable to the number of people served, making them flexible enough for a day-to-day operation where numbers may change.

With the purchase of supplies on a daily basis, smaller operators are able to impose controls by purchasing in exact quantities. Where buying advantages exist and storage facilities are available, the same control is established if the kitchen administrator retains control of supplies and issues them to the kitchen on a daily basis. Though restrictive, such controls are sometimes necessary where personnel capabilities are limited.

Order Form 1.

Order List Estimate for Kitchen No. ____
Location: Work Camp 25, Sierra Madre Mountains
Date _____
For Week of ____ to _____
Average No. of Workers _____
Average No. of Supervisors _____
Recipe Schedule for the Week _____

Aside from stock orders for regulated needs which are ordered separately, the use of Order Form 1 is all that is required to order the ingredients for a weekly period. The central commissary will compute the quantities needed and then proceed to fill the order in accordance with the week's schedule of recipes according to the series number. An established amount of over-run is allowed in each case to take care of shrinkage, which is not always controllable, and a minimum of production errors and waste. The labor production cost cannot be accurately considered for comparison. Sometimes the food is prepared by inmates and sometime by hired labor. The raw food cost of $0.3945 per meal, which includes foods grown at the Wayside Honor Farm and those purchased, compares in quality and quantity to those purchased already prepared from contract restaurants in emergencies at $1.50 per meal and where the producing restaurant has a raw food cost of $.60 per meal or 40 percent.

Beef Stew

(Yield: Approximately 5 Gallons for 100 Units of Feeding for Males on Outside Work Detail.)

Beef cut in 1-in cubes	33 lbs
Salt	1 cup
Pepper	¼ cup
Potatoes, carrots, and onions, cut	25 lbs
Brown gravy made from basic recipe	3 gal.

Method: Brown meat cubes in cooking fat and bake at 375 degrees until tender. Add salt and pepper after cooking. Boil vegetables until done and drain. Combine vegetables and meat. Add hot brown gravy and mix.

Service: For an individual portion serve 6 ounces meat with 6 ounces vegetables, 3 ounces gravy, 2 slices bread, and 7 ounces coffee with sugar.

Table 7.
Daily Minimum Food Allotment for Male under Restrictive Detention

Meal	Food	Portion
Breakfast	Cereal, dry	6 ounces
	Eggs	2
	Potatoes	4 ounces
	Coffee	7 ounces
Midday	Meat	3 ounces
	Vegetables	4 ounces
	Potatoes	3 ounces
	Bread	2 slices
	Coffee or Milk	7 ounces
Evening	Sandwich	2-ounce filling
	Pie	4-ounce slice
	or Fruit	1 piece
	Coffee or Milk	7 ounces

Table 8.
Daily Minimum Food Allotment for Male
on Outside Work Detail*

Meal	Food	Portion
Breakfast	Cereal	6 ounces
	Eggs	2
	Potatoes	4 ounces
	Coffee	7 ounces
Midday	Meat	6 ounces
	Vegetables	4 ounces
	Potatoes	4 ounces
	Fruit	1 piece
	Bread	2 slices
	Coffee or Milk	7 ounces
Evening	Sandwich	2-ounce filling
	Pie	4-ounce slice
	or Fruit	1 piece
	Coffee or Milk	7 ounces

*Work details have one rest break during both morning and afternoon and each man is allotted 7 ounces of coffee and one piece of fruit-filled pie or one sweet roll in each such period.

4.

Portioning Program Adaptable to Special Feeding Units

The criteria established by the United States Department of Agriculture (USDA) for the Type A School Lunch Program amount to a highly flexible plan for feeding situations where only minimum portions are required to meet basic needs. In brochures available from the Agriculture Department the program is described as "a beautiful picture of what a balanced meal should be," for it emphasizes an approach which is nutritionally, psychologically, and aesthetically oriented. This inclusive program is based on the logical assumption that food has no value unless it is consumed, and that if the visual and taste factors are weak, any other value is drastically reduced. These built-in standards make the program equally effective for use in homes for the aged where older people, just as young children, sometimes must be coaxed into eating by the attractiveness of what is offered. The same feature makes it useful in cafeterias or other in-plant feeding units serving sedentary workers.

The program is equally adaptable to small units such as rest homes, or for massive school feeding programs such as that of the Los Angeles Unified School District, where 250,000 meals a day come from kitchens which mass-produce tray and box lunches in a number of centrally located commissary centers for dispatch to the individual schools. The program provides for imaginative applications of a general meal pattern so that each meal provides one-third of the necessary nutrients for a growing child or the sustaining needs of the elderly or ill.

21

The sole standard of the program is that each lunch supplied under the federally endowed USDA Type A Lunch Program must include 2 ounces of protein in the form of meat, poultry, cheese, fish, eggs, beans, or peas; 1 teaspoon fresh dairy butter; ½ cup fruit; ½ cup vegetable; not less than 2 ounces of wheat or enriched bread; and ¾ cup of fresh or reconstituted dry milk solids. Slightly smaller amounts are indicated for use at preschool level and slightly larger amounts are required at the secondary level.

The individual kitchen thus has wide latitude in implementing the program. The options available in providing the protein alone are nearly countless, encouraging not only versatility in selection but also the manner of preparation.

To arrive at costs for this type of program, the USDA formula can be applied in dealing with fluctuating costs. This is done by eliminating some of the costly protein foods and replacing them with equally nutritious ones costing less money. For example: the use of whitefish fillets instead of halibut or tuna, or the occasional use of peanut butter instead of cold meats. The reimbursable cost allowance set by the government for schools adopting the program originally ranged from $.35 to $.50 per meal which, according to national surveys, covered the actual cost of the ingredients. The most any school district has had to contribute to make up for increases since the program began in 1946 has been $.15 per unit, making the maximum increase in costs of a controlled formula 30 percent in 25 years, with cost increases since 1968 rising less than 5 percent.

In homes for the aged and convalescent units, both of which are becoming more numerous, the pattern of portions established in the Type A program can be used as a guideline for creating production formulas yielding portions of a similar quantity. The food needs of the active child are comparable to those of an aged or sick person, and these portions furnish one-third of the daily nutritional requirements. Creating a series of food formulas for each of the three daily feeding schedules could also result in a control system. Just as in the controls outlined in the preceeding chapter on institutional feeding, such formulas, once established, require only that ingredients be added to or deducted from the master formula to fit the needs of the number of people to be served.

5.

The Dietetic Approach to Portioning

Los Angeles County has a published guide which can be used to adjust portions to fit any given institutional situation. The accompanying chart from the guide, when used with any calorie content scale, allows for adjusting the amounts of food needed to comprise reasonable portions. These figures are for the total daily needs in each category, making the adjustment of the amount of food to be furnished in a single meal simple and direct. Under most operating conditions, breakfast and luncheon quantities will be lower than dinner quantities except in some cases where men are assigned to heavy working conditions; in these circumstances a heavier breakfast will be needed for proper nourishment and strength.

The series of modified tables given here were issued primarily for use in schools, day care homes, and nursing homes for the elderly, but are adjustable to almost any kind of portioning where the minimum amount of nutritional food is to be served. They do not require the skills of a trained dietitian to administer or supervise. They are simple guide lines to be used where trained professional attention is not called for.

Calories and Meal Composition
Required by Adults

An approximate daily need for calories for adults can be arrived at by taking the average body weight for a person's height as given in any standard height-weight table and multiplying it by 15 for an inactive person or by 20 for an active person. These figures will not be valid for the aged, the ill, or a confined person. A dietitian will break down the needs of such people in accordance with their activities and needs in a somewhat more relevant manner as follows:

Sleeping, 8 hours:
    8 x 0.4 calories = 3.2 calories per pound
Sitting quietly without activity, 8 hours:
    8 x 0.6 calories = 4.8 calories per pound
Light activity such as walking, standing, or doing light chores, 6 hours:
    6 x 1.0 calories = 6 calories per pound
Active muscular exercise such as jogging, light coordinated work or physical therapy involving body response:
    2 x 2.0 calories = 4 calories per pound
Total calories per pound for 24 hours = 18 calories per pound

By this standard, a person whose height and body frame should weigh 150 pounds will require 2,700 calories per day (18 x 150).

In addition, the meal composition for a moderately active person should be adjusted to reflect the following proportions of foods:

Fats	45 percent
Carbohydrates	40 percent
Protein	15 percent

Table 9.
Daily Caloric Intakes

Age (years)	Activity	Sex	Calories
1-3	moderate	both	1,200
4-6	moderate	both	1,600
7-9	moderate	both	2,000
10-12	moderate	both	2,500
13-15	moderate	female	2,800
		male	3,200
16-20	moderate	female	2,800
		male	3,800
over 20	sedentary	female	2,250
		male	2,500
	active	female	2,750
		male	3,250
	very active	female	3,200
		male	4,550
	strenuous	female	3,800
		male	5,000

6.

The Mechanics of Portioning

The ultimate measure of a portion control program is how successfully it is adhered to at the point of service. If the correct amounts of food are placed on the plate, the program works.

In the commercial restaurant service will most frequently be performed by trained personnel in the cook or subcook category. In most institutions, however, serving will be performed by less experienced personnel who will need thorough instruction in portioning and placement of food on the serving plate.

A combination of skills which will both control the amounts and appearance of food on the plate can be achieved by instructing serving personnel to place the food on the center of the plate, well off the rim. Only a limited amount of food can be placed in the circle, making both overloading and sloppy arrangement obvious to the supervisor. Figure 3 shows food placed properly and improperly.

In assembly line procedures of serving it is especially important that plates be properly balanced with the correct amount of food, which is the cost control feature, as well as an aesthetic concern. Each plate should leave the assembly line with exactitude in quantity and eye appeal.

Where the free dipping system is used (serving bulk foods from a warming table pan or from insert pans), serving spoons and dippers in graded sizes should be used with gravies or sauces; slotted for draining off liquids completely; perforated for partially draining off liquids. They come in capacities of 1, 2, or 3 ounces. Long handled ladles are

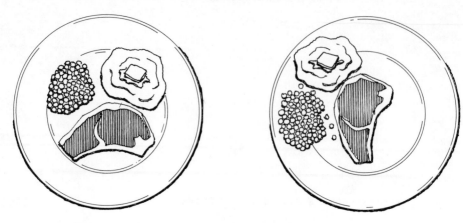

Fig. 3. *Aesthetic placement of food vs. food placed sloppily on rim of plate.*

more flexible, coming in graduated capacities of from 1 to 16 ounces. Ice cream dippers can also be used; they come in graduated sizes of from 1/8 to 1/2 cup capacity. (See Table 12.) By providing the correct-size dipper for each item to be served, supervisors can be assured that foods are being served in controlled, predetermined portions.

In the production kitchen, portioning takes on more aspects than the mere weighing of food. Steaks, cutlets, or chops in their raw form should be measured by marking off a primal cut of meat, regardless of

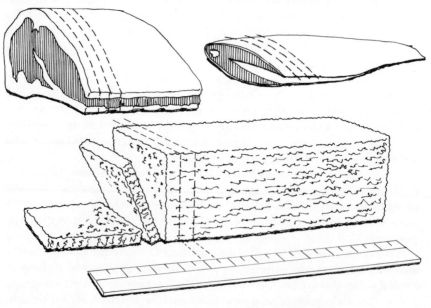

Fig. 4. *Portioning raw food by the "measuring method."*

its weight, to produce a given number of portions as shown in Figure 4. This can also be done with hams, meat loaves, whole fish or fletches, or with any other mass of food. In each case a predetermined number of orders will be made from the whole and the actual weight of each portion will be disregarded.

For portioning bulk quantities in the kitchen, there are measured paper cups, fluted paper souffle cups, ramikins, baking dishes, and casseroles. Ice cream scoops of different sizes can be used for measuring sandwich fillings and cottage cheese or for forming meat balls or portions of ground meats to be flattened into patties. (Figure 5 shows some examples of serving ladles and dippers.)

Table 12.
Size of Dipper or Scoop
and Equivalents

Dipper No.	Measure	Yield per Quart
8	1/2 cup or 8 tablespoons	6-1/2
10	2/5 cups or 6 tablespoons	7-1/2 to 8
12	1/4 cup +	12
16	1/5 cup +	13-1/2
20	1/5 cup +	16-1/2
24	1/6 cup	20
30	1/8 cup or 2 tablespoons	23

With ramikins or various other forms of baking dishes, foods can be preportioned and held in the warming table for convenient and rapid serving or stored under refrigeration and heated to meet demands. In this way portioning can be accomplished in a controlled, orderly fashion, rather than haphazardly at the point of service.

The various kinds of portioning scales run from simple ounce scales to sophisticated "over-and-under" scales. Obviously, a scale is an absolute necessity for accurate portioning.

Cutting guide markers are available for 8- and 9-inch pies and cakes. They vary in the number of slices allowed. Also available are aluminum baking dishes for one-time use. These come in an array of sizes to fit almost any situation, making them one of the better methods for controlling amounts of food to be cooked in them and served direct to the consumer. Figure 6 shows some methods of portioning cakes.

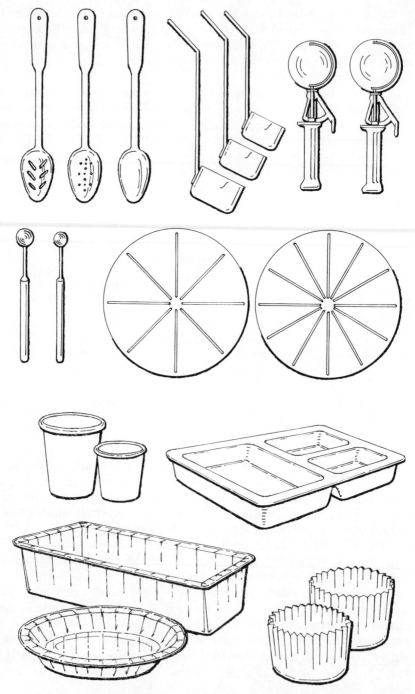

Fig. 5. *Portioning bulk quantities with various measuring devices.*

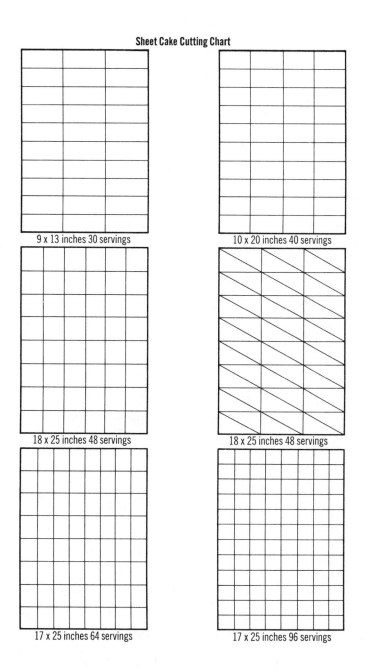

Fig. 6. *Cake cutting charts in various forms and sizes.*

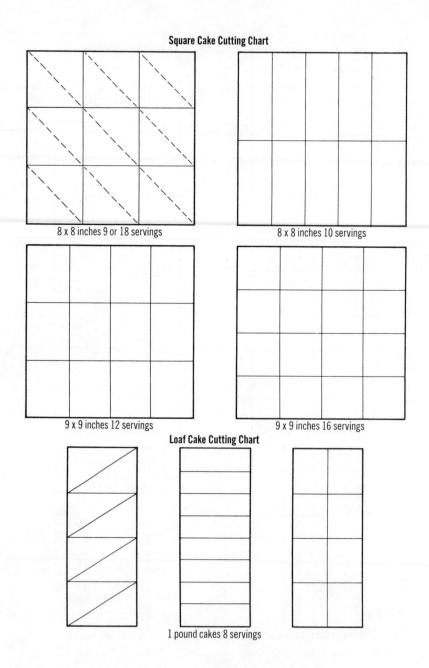

Square Cake Cutting Chart

8 x 8 inches 9 or 18 servings

8 x 8 inches 10 servings

9 x 9 inches 12 servings

9 x 9 inches 16 servings

Loaf Cake Cutting Chart

1 pound cakes 8 servings

Fig. 6. *Cake cutting charts in various forms and sizes.*

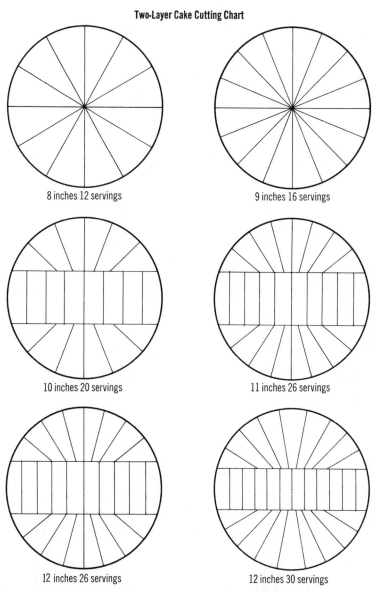

Two-Layer Cake Cutting Chart

8 inches 12 servings

9 inches 16 servings

10 inches 20 servings

11 inches 26 servings

12 inches 26 servings

12 inches 30 servings

Three-layer cakes should be cut in the same manner as shown above. However, reduce the size of each serving approximately one-third in order to increase the number of servings.

Fig. 6. *Cake cutting charts in various forms and sizes.*

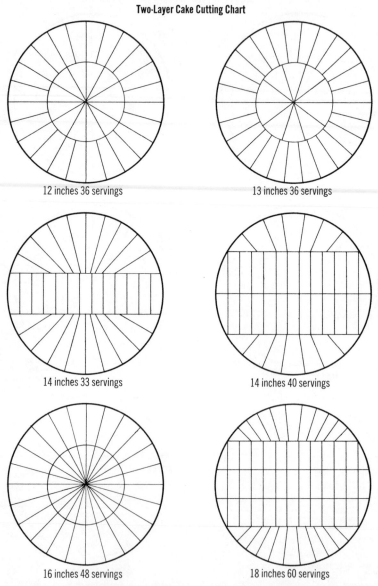

Two-Layer Cake Cutting Chart

12 inches 36 servings

13 inches 36 servings

14 inches 33 servings

14 inches 40 servings

16 inches 48 servings

18 inches 60 servings

Three-layer cakes should be cut in the same manner as shown above. However, reduce the size of each serving approximately one-third in order to increase the number of servings.

Fig. 6. *Cake cutting charts in various forms and sizes.*

7.

The Summing-Up of Portion Control

No attempt at establishing a portion control program will prove successful without close attention to the needs, demands, and tastes of the specific group your institution will serve. These vary, as we have established, depending on age level, degree of activity, status of health, and freedom of movement. In designing and imposing a portion control program, one must allow for initial adjustments in arriving at suitable fixed portions.

In the absence of exact clinical or academic information about how various categories of persons should be considered in arriving at correct portions, Tables 13 and 14 give examples of practical amounts to meet three types of feeding. (In almost exact conformity to these figures, at least two major food processors have recently introduced complete lines of frozen dinners to fit these same situations.) The commercial restaurant can be used as a standard for adult feeding, for it must supply satisfying portions to maintain its trade. Insufficient portions will drive customers away and portions which are too large will kill profits. This same need for balance applies to budgeted institutions as well, for money is usually allocated in accordance with well-defined feeding situations.

In the program developed for the Los Angeles County Sheriff's Department Detention Facilities, there is a stipulated allowance of $0.3945 per person per meal for the cost of feeding. But, although the allowance is identical from institution to institution, the feeding situations are not. In each instance the kitchen producing the food will apply a prescribed series of menu items; the food to produce them in varying portions is dispatched from the central commissary. Thus, a facility producing food for detained juveniles will offer menus differing from that producing food for adult males or for adult females. And within these distinctions are even further adjustments based on the degrees of inmate activity. Savings made on the basic foods supplied facilities serving smaller portions will be passed on to those where larger portions are dispensed.

Table 13.
Variations in Amounts and Costs of
Portions for Meat Loaf*

Dinner Service in Rest Home for the Aged		*Dinner Service for Counter Operation of Coffee Shop or Diner*	
Meat loaf, 3 ounces @ $0.0705	= $.225	Meat loaf, 6 ounces @ $0.0750	= $.45
Potatoes, 2 ounces @ $.01	= $.02	Gravy or sauce	= $.05
Vegetable, 3 ounces @ $.03	= $.09	Potatoes, 3 ounces@ $.01	= $.03
1 slice bread and butter	= $.05	Vegetable, 3 ounces @ $.03	= $.09
3 ounces dessert	= $.10	Salad or soup	= $.15
Coffee or milk	= $.10	Bread or roll and butter	= $.10
		Beverage	a la carte

*The quantity produced will be 6 loaves weighing 1 pound each with ingredients costing $7.27.

Luncheon Service for Inplant Facility
Catering to Employees Engaged in Sedentary Work

Meat loaf, 4 ounces @ $0.0750	= $.30
Sauce or gravy	= $.05
Vegetable, 3 ounces @ $.03	= $.09
Bread or roll and butter	= $.10
Fruit compote or Desert	= $.10
Beverage a la carte	= $.10

Table 14.

Variations in Amounts and Costs of Portions in Preparing Beef and Vegetable Stew Meal*

Service for School Cafeteria Children Ages 10 - 15	*Service for Restaurant Luncheon*	*Service for Detention Feeding (Inactive Male)*	*Service for Detention Feeding (Active Male)*
Portion: 1 cup (½ pint)	Portion: 1 bowl (¾ pint)	Portion: 1 soup cup (½ pint)	Portion: 1 large bowl 1 (pint)
Formula yield: 84 portions @ $.19	Formula yield: 63 portions @ $0.2850	Formula yield: 84 portions @ $.19	Formula yield: 42 portions @ $.38

*The quantity produced will be 5½ gallons with ingredients costing $16.00. Each portion would also include 4 crackers and ½ pint of milk for school children; 2 slices of bread, 2 pats of butter, and beverage for detention feeding; and would be served on a bed of steamed rice or boiled noodles plus 2 slices of bread, 1 pat of butter, and beverage for restaurant service.

Each active male also receives dessert.

Thus we see that food prepared from a production formula for a fixed amount of money will have varying values as far as income and budgeting are concerned; and that this holds true for both restaurants and nonprofit institutions. If the kitchen prepares the food by a formula for active adults when it is feeding children or the aged, overproduction will occur. Formulas for the young or the aged, conversely, will not be sufficient to provide for the same number of adults.

The kitchen manager, therefore, must use his administrative abilities to determine what, if any, adjustment is needed in a recipe before it goes into production. In the beginning there may be a certain amount of trial and error, especially if the number of people to be fed from a recipe varies, as in the case of a commercial restaurant. To experiment in arriving at correct quantities, it is best to use foods which can be stored under refrigeration and used at another time, or those which will combine with other foods to create a different product. The prevention of waste from overproduction is paramount if the cost control program is to function with precision.

To sum up, the ultimate goal in portion control is to place the correct amount of food on a plate for a particular situation at a known and controllable cost. Furthermore, it should be the maximum amount and quality of food possible within the price allowance structure.

8.

Forecast Buying

The system of forecasting food purchases to take advantage of lows in a price cycle for use during peak seasons when prices are high varies from the commercial restaurant to the institution. The system, however, is valid for both types of operation. Forecast purchasing anticipates needs over a long-range period and allows for buying in a depressed market for delivery as the foods are required. This purchasing method is known as "future contracts," a system used by practically all large organizations in the food industry. The price at delivery will be that agreed to at the time of purchase, plus charges for handling, storage, taxes, processing and interest. The total cost will usually be considerably lower in many lines, especially in steak meat prices which rise during summer months. Future contracts not only result in savings but also insure the stability of the cost control program.

Future buying is practiced extensively with frozen products. Seafoods, processed meats, vegetables, and fruits are always at the low end of their price cycle at processing time, which coincides with their peak of quality. The small operator can take advantage of the savings in the same manner as the larger buyer since there is no financial outlay at the time of purchase, only the obligation that the restaurant take delivery of the material within a given period of time. The purveyor will provide storage space at a cost below that which a restaurant would invest in its own facility. This is a decided plus for businesses of all sizes.

Overbuying has its evils, whether it be in long-range purchasing or daily guesswork. However, there is security available in the former; an arrangement can be made at the time of purchase in which the purveyor will continue to hold the merchandise beyond the stated period.

There will, of course, be the added expenses of storage and interest, a drawback that may escalate the delivery price sufficiently to wipe out anticipated savings.

To eliminate as much over-buying (or under-buying) as possible, accurate forecasting is a must and is one of management's most important functions. For new organizations this amounts to intelligent guess work, while the experienced operator is able to review and analyze the previous year's purchases. The forecast can then proceed, taking future business fluctuations into consideration. Since the delivery of the merchandise sometimes does not begin for the better part of a year and in quantities to supply yet another year, the true time span may actually extend to a final delivery date as much as two years ahead in extreme cases. This makes forecasting a difficult procedure.

Tables 15, 16, and Order Form 2. are used for forecasting by Transudan Associates of Los Angeles, contract operators of medium-sized coffee shop-dining room operations. Tables 15 and 16 show how the

Table 15.
Breakdown of Food Cost Dollar for
Purchases Made June to September*

Item	*Percentage of Food Cost Dollar*
Meats	24
Poultry	8
Seafoods	12
Produce	15
Potatoes	2
Eggs	3
Dairy products	12
Coffee	2
Grocery staples	14
Bakery products	6
Misc.	2

Amount of purchases for
same period of previous year $_____

*Used in cost forecasting by Transudan Associates of Los Angeles

company makes a study of the merchandise situation for the previous year; then by adding any anticipated growth percentage, they can make projections for future needs for each unit, adding a slight overrun for contingencies.

Once the amounts are determined, Table 17 is used to request bids. The quotation form carries a request for the current price and the delivered price during the stipulated period, including processing, freezing, storing, and interest charges. This gives the operators a two-fold approach to buying. If the delivered price promises to exceed the anticipated market price they can purchase directly with the aid of bank loans, then seek bids for processing and storage in an attempt to lower delivery costs. If the price is acceptable, they can contract directly with the purveyor and let him assume those responsibilities.

Table 16.
Category Breakdown of Items Purchased*

Item	*Percentage*
Meats	
Boneless chuck	24
Strip loins	8
Ground beef patties, 4 ounces	28
Veal cutlets	
4 ounces	8
3 ounces	4
Ribs, primal	5
Prefab. steak sandwich, cubed	
4 ounces	18
Variety meats	5
Seafoods	
Shrimp	
under 8 per pound	6
12-16 per pound	40
broken	4
Sole fillets	
individually frozen pieces	20
5-pound solid pack	30

*Used in cost forecasting by Transudan Associates of Los Angeles

Table 16.
Category Breakdown of Items Purchased* *(Continued)*

Item	Percentage
Poultry	
Friers, 2-2½ pounds	60
Stewing hens, heavy	20
Turkeys, 28-32 pounds	20
Produce	
Perishables	80
Frozen, misc.	20
Potatoes	
frozen, precut, blanched, 3/8 inch	80
canned flakes	20
Groceries	
Misc. staples	80
String beans, under No. 6	
sieve, No. 10 cans	10
Peas, large colored,	
No. 10 cans	10

*Used in cost forecasting by Transudan Associates of Los Angeles

In using forecast purchasing for meats, early delivery will not affect the price. Usually the purveyor will set his delivered price on a per pound basis, as long as delivery is made within the contracted period. Thus the purchaser will have a fixed price throughout the term of the agreement.

Institutional forecasting patterns are different from those of restaurants. The detention facility, for example, will have an occupancy pattern closely relating to the seasons; during summer periods they will most often be taxed to their limits. Rest homes for the aged will have peaks in winter months when sickness is more common among the elderly, while school cafeterias must adjust to vacation periods. The common denominator for all is that forecasting is based on the anticipated number of people to be fed, using the daily basic needs for one individual and multiplying it by the expected peak for any given season.

Forecast purchasing of foods other than meat offers different conditions and advantages. Canned and frozen produce usually comes not from one purveyor but from many. This makes forecasting more complex and time-consuming. To further complicate matters, such produce is often drop-shipped directly from the processor rather than being delivered by the purveyors. The drop-shipping system does not allow for close coordination with current needs; the purchaser must instead expect delivery at the processor's convenience; the latter may choose to ship when he needs to clear his storage facilities and/or when he finds it advantageous to route a shipment in a particular direction.

Order Form 2.
Request for Quotation*

Item	Purchased Price per Pound	Delivered Price per Pound	Date
1000 pounds strip loins USDA Choice. Delivery between June and September. Cryovaced and frozen.			
1200 boxes, 3 pounds each. Veal cutlets, 4 ounce. Packed 12 to the box with individual separators and frozen. Delivery between June and September.			
Ground beef patties, 4 ounces, 15/20 percent fat content maximum. Packed in 50 pound boxes with individual separators. Delivery 1000-1200 pounds monthly between June and October, inclusive.			

*Used for bid requests by Transudan Associates of Los Angeles

Furthermore, produce purchase, unlike meats, does not typically involve long-term contracts; the timespan between purchase and delivery is relatively short. Therefore one most often simply pays the price agreed to at the time of purchase. Under most circumstances only those goods used in quantity are purchased in this manner—and then only those with a high consumption rate over a short timespan.

What *are* the advantages of purchasing bulk canned or frozen foods on a forecast basis? Aside from the obvious benefit of buying at a known, fixed price, one may also be assured of having at hand those fancy grade goods that may only be packed in season and are otherwise unavailable. Large green peas, whole tiny green beans, pearl onions, number one size peas, whole small beets, whole small carrots, whole small new potatoes, and other items that require special grading, sizing, or coloring will not be generally available year-round. The packer will usually forewarn that when an existing supply is depleted, no more will be available until the next special packing. In some circumstances, a packer may only process enough of a special type of product to meet forecast contract obligations, usually when the product is not in great general demand.

Although each packing company has its own policies, sometimes making it difficult for the buyer to find the correct source of supply, wholesale supply houses catering to the institutional market will usually be able to act as advisors or agents.

Contract buying of canned merchandise, especially vegetables, offers assurance that items will be supplied exactly as specified, even though delivery is not always convenient. Merchandise in varying grades will sometimes be packed only when there is an available abundant supply and an attractive price.

Open market meat buying at wholesale levels is often a problem for the smaller organization. To interest a wholesaler in his business, the small buyer should plan to consolidate his meat orders to reduce the number of deliveries. Frequent, small deliveries are the bane of meat sellers. Most dealers have a break-even point which requires orders to exceed $50.00; for lesser amounts often result in an actual loss. This is an important issue to resolve because most meat plants are geared to a standard method of production which if interrupted by small special orders will result in an operating loss. If standard cuts and sizes are ordered, they can be produced on an assembly line where the meat is broken down uniformly, making the cost to each customer, no matter the size of the order, the same.

Basically, the purveyor can offer two types of service to the small institution. He will prepare cuts and pieces to specification, with price based on the finished product. Here the purveyor absorbs the cost of the resulting trim. The other service involves a cut-and-send process, where the cuts will be trimmed according to specification from a gross amount of meat, with the resulting trim also sent along to the buyer. The quoted price will be for the primal cut with a possible small processing charge added. This service will be the more economical, providing the buyer can utilize the trim.

Because the small buyer will make more specific demands upon the purveyor per dollar spent than will the larger buyer, the former should avoid shopping among several suppliers. Any savings achieved this way will be small, especially when measured against the restricted services he will receive. The wholesale meat business is highly competitive; almost without exception the buyer can expect comparable prices and better service if he gives all his meat business to one reliable dealer. To find such a dealer, a certain amount of checking and shopping may be necessary. Once found, however, he should be allowed to provide for the needs of the institution. When a wholesaler gets the "feel" of an institution and begins to understand its requirements, he will be best suited to supply those products with a high degree of suitability for the production kitchen. Although one may pay a slightly higher cost per pound, if the merchandise is economical in its application an actual savings will result.

9.

Meat Buying

More than any other aspect of the buying program, meat purchasing requires knowledge and a deep sense of responsibility. Meat buying must be a part of the portion and production programs, the goal being a synchronized set of specifications spelling out exactly the types and grades of product to be purchased though the meat may be used in a variety of menus. The preportioned hamburger patty for example may appear on the restaurant menu as a hamburger sandwich patty, a patty-melt hamburger and cheese sandwich, a lo-cal luncheon plate, or a child's dinner plate. Establishing a uniform specification for the size of the patty involves the simultaneous act of establishing a portion control and a recipe with a built-in cost control.

In buying bulk items such as boneless chuck or beef rounds the meat buying specifications should take into account the advantages of by-products which might result from certain trimming and weigh them against the advantages of purchasing meat in ready-to-use form. To create buying specifications the purchaser will need to be thoroughly familiar with the specifics of kitchen production and the established quality standards. Also necessary is a knowledge of the talents and capabilities of the staff. Do they have the skill to portion primal cuts with the same efficiency as the purveyor who will employ experts? Just as important is the need to understand the production potential of the available kitchen equipment if meat portioning is to be economical and efficient.

Tables 17 and 18 are typical of forms used by the kitchen for ordering meats from the buyer where a set specification has been es-

46

Table 17.
Single-Unit Check List for a
Commercial Restaurant*

Day Required	Production Needs	Anticipated Portions	Amount Required
6/18	Boneless chuck USDA standard (braised beef stew)	300 @ 4 portions per pound	75 pounds
6/18	Ground beef, 20 percent fat content (meat loaf)	100 @ 5 portions per pound	20 pounds
6/18	Ground beef patties, 4 ounce (for stock use)	1000	250 pounds

*This simple form can be used for direct ordering since all items have been predetermined by production specifications, making consideration of by-products unnecessary.

Table 18.
Meat Requisition for Storage Purposes*

Item	Normal Weekly Build-up	On Hand	Need
Boneless chuck USDA Commercial	1000 pounds	200 pounds	800 pounds
Lamb legs	12	3	9
Veal cutlets, 4 ounce	100 pounds	10 pounds	90 pounds
Hamburger patties, 4 ounce	500 pounds	100 pounds	400 pounds
Beef livers	10	3	7

*This form serves as a weekend inventory as well as a purchase request for the ensuing week. It works where a product is in continuous use, with the build-up figure set to accommodate business fluctuations.

tablished for daily and weekly open market purchasing. In both instances the kitchen program has been synchronized with the buying program in such a manner that consultation is not necessary. In each case the buyer will be able to place orders for the merchandise exactly as ordered.

Where organizations use standardized food formulas for production, such recipes have usually been created with specific requirements for the meats needed in their preparation. The buying program is thus systematized and only those specific cuts and grade need to be considered. In open market purchasing the buying program is only a matter of placing the orders as they are received from the kitchen and done as frequently as necessary.

In smaller organizations with limited storage space, overbuying of perishable products will create losses. To avoid this, many such organizations buy frozen products or freeze those on hand when surpluses accumulate. Although there exists a certain negative attitude toward frozen meats, they are finding ever expanding acceptance by institutions. The handling and cooking of frozen meats is discussed in detail in the second section of this book along with their advantages. For now let it suffice that the system detailed here could not be exploited to any extent without the use of the freezing process.

For all purchasing needs, those items which are traditionally frozen at the time of production must be considered. A large percentage of veal is available only in frozen form. Likewise a great amount of lamb and many pork products are only available frozen. Most portioned meats such as veal cutlets, pork cutlets, cube steaks, laminated beef steaks and chicken parts are also only sold this way. All are products of importance in an institutional feeding program.

The buying program that looks no farther ahead than a day or a week will be the victim of price cycles endemic to the wholesale food supply business, a situation brought about by fluctuations in supply and demand. The method of simple future buying can serve as a price stabilizer. In addition, however, in order to purchase the proper grade of such items as meat or canned vegetable when future buying, it is necessary to know and understand the different grading levels as established by the Agriculture Department. These grades are explained in the following evaluation of beef and canned vegetables.

Comparative Evaluation of Beef Grades

The following information is based on grades published by the United States Department of Agriculture.

USDA Prime Grade

As its name implies, this is the top quality of meat available in the market. It is produced from young, specially fed cattle under controlled conditions. The marbling effect of the fat interspersed throughout the lean portions results in juiciness, tenderness, and intense flavor when properly cooked. Because of its excessive fat a large amount of trim is characteristic, adding to the cost of the ready-to-cook product beyond the original price per pound.

USDA Choice Grade

This grade is produced in greater quantities than the Prime Grade beef, is more abundant in the market at a lower price level, contains less marbling and general overall fat but retains a high place on the scale of palatability, tenderness, and juiciness. The well-developed flavor extends to all cuts, though a certain amount of waste develops where primal cuts are altered to produce certain by-products such as short-ribs or rolled chuck roasts.

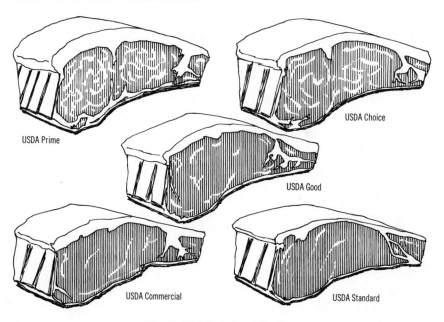

Fig. 7. *U.S.D.A. Beef Grades.*

USDA Good Grade

This grade has a high degree of quality and will have less fat than the upper grades, making it somewhat less juicy. Marbling will be less predominant, resulting in the meat having a higher proportion of lean. It will have a relative degree of tenderness and flavor which is less than the Choice grade because it is not quite as heavy with fat covering and marbling. It will produce less trim when broken down into various cuts for utility purposes.

USDA Standard Grade

This grade has a very thin covering of fat and very little marbling, giving it a high percentage of lean meat. It will usually lack the tenderness of the upper grades but lends itself well to methods of preparation which will tenderize the meat while cooking. The flavor is mild. Very little trim results in breaking the meat down into usable parts.

USDA Commercial Grade

This grade is usually produced from older cattle. It is lacking in tenderness but flavor will be mature and robust. It lends itself to long, slow methods of cooking which makes this grade of meat develop rich, full beef characteristics. Little fat and a high degree of lean meat, make this grade satisfactory for producing economical meat-based dishes where flavor will be released into sauces and accompaning extenders.

USDA Utility, Canner, and Cutter Grades

These grades are generally unavailable in the market or as fresh beef. They come from cattle in advanced age so that the meat is principally used in processed products.

Comparative Evaluation of Canned Vegetable Grades

U.S. Grade A or Fancy

This grade is top quality merchandise selected for size, color, and maturity at the peak of perfection.

U.S. Grade B or Choice

This grade is not as uniform in size, color, or maturity as Grade A, but is of high quality.

U.S. Grade C or Standard

This grade is random packed as to size, color, and maturity. The quality is good but the appearance will vary from packing to packing. Standard is usually that merchandise remaining after the two upper grades have been selected.

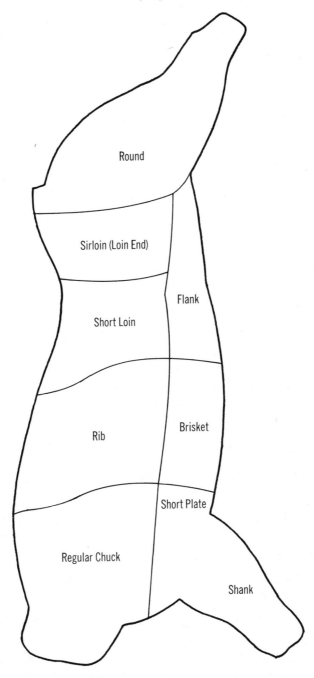

Fig. 8. *Beef chart (wholesale cuts).*

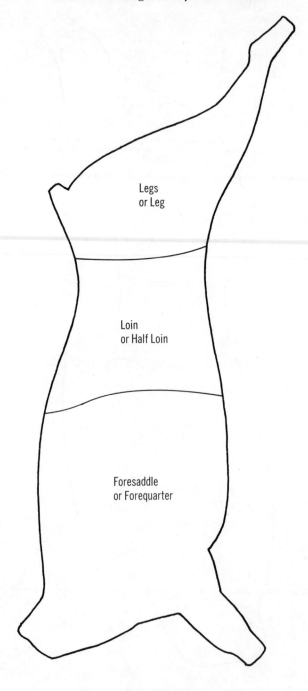

Fig. 9. *Veal chart (wholesale cuts).*

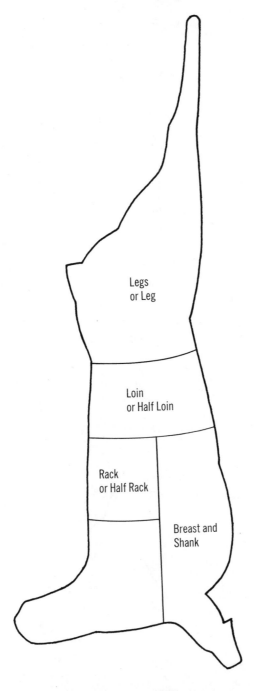

Fig. 10. *Lamb chart (wholesale cuts).*

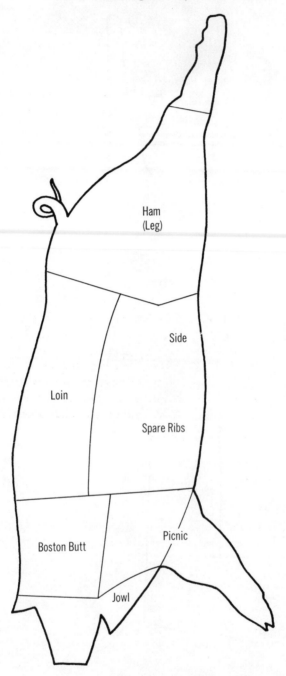

Fig. 11. *Pork chart (wholesale cuts).*

10.

Buying Seafoods

Open market purchasing of some seafood items in nationwide short supply has become difficult since a steady source needs to be maintained. This condition is further aggravated because there is a reluctance on the part of some purveyors to respond favorably to entering into forecast buying contracts where a stipulated delivery price will be established. This is especially true in the case of shrimp, lobsters, or crabs. These same purveyors will, however, make contracts for a guaranteed delivery of a stipulated quantity but only at the prevailing market price at the time the delivery is made. There remains certain advantages in this method of buying beyond the assurance of delivery. Primarily, deliveries are usually arranged to coincide with the periods of peak production or catch when the market prices are at the low in the price cycle. Most purveyors who buy heavily have limited storage facilities and need to move merchandise rapidly in order to operate competitively. Secondly, storage costs and interest on their merchandise investments do not accumulate since the purveyor moves the merchandise at the time of receipt from the producer and deals on a short-time cash basis with the buyer. These factors being common to all purveyors at the time have a tendency to put delivered prices on a competitive basis. All purveyors will be under equal pressure at the time of periodic heavy harvests.

Where a purveyor is under contract to deliver merchandise, those having made prior agreements are serviced first with any remaining merchandise sold in the open market or stored. This can in a manner be compared to drop shipments of other types of food since the purveyor will sometimes only tranship the products from the processor to the user, acting as a middle man for distribution and sale.

Many purveyors who still enter into forecast agreements on items which are traditionally in short supply are less inclined to work on a narrow margin as they do with other items. Most insist on contingency clauses which will cover them on fluctuating interest rates and other unforeseen charges for storage and for handling. All require a stipulated delivery date to assure that all merchandise contracted for will be accepted by the buyer during the life term of the agreement. To cover chances of loss they insist on the posting of a performance bond by the buyer or a sizeable advance payment at the time the agreement is negotiated. This arrangement ensures a source but it does not create a static delivery price as in forecast purchasing of other merchandise, though in most cases price advantages will exist.

Seafoods have recently fallen into the same position (and will apparently remain there) where purveyors will not contract for items in short supply such as crabs, lobsters, and especially lobster tails. Most sellers continue to enter into regular forecast agreements for all other items which sometimes have temporary volatile periods of price increases due to sporadic seasonal demand or availability such as halibut, sea bass, and some popular varieties of sole. By having an established price in contractural purchasing where the ceiling will be limited and where supply is assured, seasonal problems can be avoided. The use of low-cost items such as steak cod, haddock, or yellowtail flounders in place of more costly and sometimes seasonally scarce items eliminates the need for advance buying because there items are always available in a stable price cycle.

Fresh water fish, as a whole, will always remain in normal supply. Many such items such as trout and catfish and other species which are popular are grown on fish farms capable of increasing production to meet demand. Some fresh water shrimp are also being produced in small lots with good prospects for the future.

Where seafood sources are localized, the best buys can be found by using what is known in the trade as "the catch of the day." This is the simple procedure of buying whatever is immediately available in abundance and adjusting the menu to fit the products purchases. This requires a certain amount of flexibility in the kitchen but it assures a low cost on prime fresh merchandise. Where freezing facilities are a part of the kitchen equipment, quality buying and quantity buying can become synonymous. Frequently this method of buying is one where the institution buyer will deal directly with the fishing vessels, bypassing the purveyor completely. Most fishermen who deal in this manner will custom dress fish to suit the buyer (see Figure 12). The cost will always be somewhat below wholesale level.

Prepacked Seafood

Unless regionally available fresh seafoods are in abundant supply at attractive prices, most institutions prefer to purchase from specialists who deal in packaging and processing techniques best suited to institutional use. Most seafoods are available frozen, although some are canned or ice packed. The latter process keeps them fresh, while allowing for shipment to distant points. Ice-packed merchandise is highly perishable, however, and must be kept under sharp refrigeration just above the freezing point and surrounded by crushed ice. Vacuum

Fig. 12. *Available forms of fresh fish—whole, drawn, dressed, steaks, and fillets.*

packed cans may be kept at normal refrigeration temperature—between 36 and 40 degrees. Frozen merchandise should be stored at below zero temperature.

When buying fresh fish it is important to be familiar with its characteristics and specifications. Fresh fish are characterized by the following good qualities:

1. The skin and color is bright with patterns well-defined.
2. The scales adhere tightly to the skin and have a bright sheen.
3. The eyes are bright, full, and bulging; avoid those with filmy covering.
4. The gills must be red or bright pink.
5. The flesh will be firm to the touch, and elastic in response to pressure.
6. Odors should be fishy but not objectionable.

The specifications of standard fresh fish are as follows:

1. *Whole Fish.* This category covers the fish just as taken, with scales, head, tail and fins intact.
2. *Drawn Fish.* The entrails have been removed, otherwise it is in the form indicated above.
3. *Dressed Fish.* The entrails, head, fins, tail and scales have been removed and the fish is ready to cook.
4. *Steaks.* These are cross sections of larger fish with side flaps removed. They are boneless except for the center backbone. Thickness can be to specific order.
5. *Fillets.* These are side strips of fish cut lengthwise and away from the backbone. They are usually boneless, and a very thin fish will have skin intact.

The packaging sizes and standards usually employed by processors for packaging seafoods are explained here:

1. Boxed Frozen Shrimp, each in 5 pound boxes:
   Large, 21-25 pieces per pound
   Jumbo, 15-20 pieces per pound
   Large jumbo, 12-15 pieces per pound
   Extra jumbo, 8-10 pieces per pound
2. Bagged and Canned Frozen Shrimp: Cocktail shrimp, various sizes peeled and deveined. Cans are No. 10; bags contain 2½ and 5 pounds
3. Scallops:
   Fresh large in 1 gallon cans, ice-packed
   Fresh small in 1 gallon cans, ice-packed
4. Frozen Scallops:
   Medium size, 5 pound packages
   Large size, 5 pound packages
5. Frozen Sole Fillets:
   I.Q.F. (individually frozen pieces) 6-8 ounces, and 8-10 ounces, each in 5 pound boxes
   Block pack, random-size pieces, 4-6 ounce pieces, 6-8 ounce pieces, and 8-10 ounce pieces, each in 5 pound boxes

6. Shelled Clams:
    Small for frying or chowders, fresh, 1 gallon can, ice-packed
    Diced or minced, frozen, 2½ or 4 pound block pack
7. Shelled Oysters:
    Standards, 325-335 per gallon, ice-packed, 1 gallon cans
    Selects, 225-235 per gallon, ice-packed, 1 gallon cans
    Extra selects, 200-225 per gallon, ice-packed, 1 gallon cans
8. Halibut:
    Whole, head off, 10-60 pounds, frozen
    Half pieces or sections, 5-10 pounds, frozen
    Steaks, 6, 8, and 10 ounces, individually frozen, each in 5 pound boxes
9. Finnan Haddie:
    Whole, 4-6 pounds, ice-packed
    Large fillets, boneless, 2½-3 pounds, ice-packed
    Jumbo fillets, boneless, 4-5 pounds, ice-packed

Table 19 lists common seafood and their respective fat contents.

Table 19.
Seafood Characteristics

Fish	*Fat Content*
Albacore (Tuna)	Fat
Barracuda	Fat
Bass, Sea	Lean
Bass, Stripped	Fat
Cod	Lean
Finnan Haddie (Haddock)	Lean
Halibut	Lean
Mackerel	Fat
Rockfish	Fat
Salmon	Fat
Sand Dabs	Lean
Shad and Shad Roe	Fat
Smelts	Fat
Sole	Lean
Sole, Rex	Fat
Squid	Fat
Trout	Fat
Turbot	Fat
Whitebait	Fat

11.

Buying Fresh Produce

In times when crops are abundant or at the peak of harvest the quality of fresh produce will be highest and the price lowest. The thinner the crop, the poorer the quality and the higher the price, making the buying of fresh produce out of season a costly gamble. The obvious and customary procedure during these unfavorable purchasing periods is to replace fresh products whenever possible with either frozen or canned items.

Among standard produce items, only potatoes can be purchased through contract or forecast buying. Even for the medium to small organization where forecast buying is not practiced, potato processors will agree to supply products over extended periods at a fixed price. Usually the only stipulation is that the buyer must purchase the products in the approximate amounts specified when the agreement is made.

Processed potatoes are available in many forms, shapes, and sizes as shown in Figure 14, making them adaptable to all kinds of use. Whole processed raw potatoes come in graded sizes and are peeled and chemically treated to prevent browning or color deterioration. They will keep well under refrigeration for from 3 to 5 days. Standard packing is in 25-pound bags. Smaller sizes come steam blanched, approximately three-quarters cooked. They can be used for slicing, grating, or cutting into pieces for various cooking purposes.

Some processors supply whole baking size potatoes with skins at graded sizes with a limit of 1 ounce tolerance. These are oven-ready, having been tumbler washed and treated with oils or coating for the

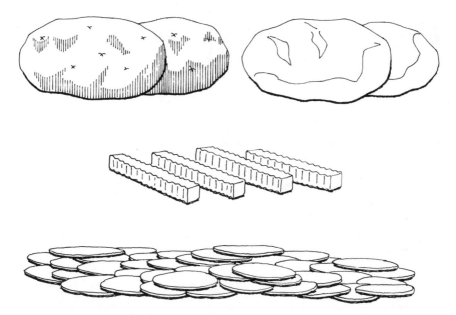

Fig. 13. *Processed raw potatoes—peeled, sliced, and grated.*

skins. Their holding period will be equal to that of fresh potatoes and they require no refrigeration.

Processed cut potatoes come in 1/4, 3/8, and 1/2 inch cuts for shoe strings or french fries, and are available either raw and chemically treated to prevent color deterioration, or steam or oil blanched, for quick cooking and grease conservation in deep fat friers. Refrigerated storage life is the same as for whole processed potatoes. These cuts are also available frozen and must be thawed before cooking. Standard packing is in 25-pound bags or boxes.

Semi-cooked grated potatoes for making hash browns are available in 5-, 10-, and 25-pound bags. These have a relatively short life under refrigeration, quite often tending to mold or deteriorate in color after 3 to 4 days. They can either be frozen in individual portions for quick use or, if stored by the bag, can be left partially thawed to facilitate portioning.

Canned potatoes or packaged dehydrated potatoes for mashing are most generally available from wholesale grocers although some potato processors carry them for the convenience of their customers. The same is true of whole small potatoes, which come water packed in number 10 cans in various sizes and grades. (For purchasing fresh potatoes and making determinations as to the grade properly suited to the need, the grade comparison given in Table 20 will be useful.)

Table 20.

Grade Comparison Chart for Potatoes

Grade	Size	Defect tolerance
U.S. Fancy*	Random pack will be 40 percent over 6 inches in length, 60 percent over 2¼ inches in diameter	6 percent total defects including maximum of 1 percent soft rot or wet break-down
U.S. No. 1*	All over 1 7/8 inches in diameter unless otherwise specified	5 percent damage by hollow heart, 6 percent from other causes including 1 percent for soft rot or wet break-dow[1]
U.S. No. 2	All over 1½ inches in diameter unless otherwise specified	Same as U.S. No. 1
U.S. Commercial	Random pack similar to U.S. No. 1 and U.S. No. 2	20 percent total defects with maximum of 5 percent serious damage

*U.S. Fancy or U.S. No. 1 available in specified sizes with a tolerance of 1/2 inch in diameter and 1 ounce in weight. Grading cost in both sizes 10 percent above market for random pack.

Onions are also available in processed form in sizes and shapes readily adaptable to general cooking procedures. Dehydrated onions come in flakes or slices, seasoned or unseasoned, packed in 1-pound packages or in number 10 cans. For cooking they are more economical than fresh onions, for processed onions have a prolonged shelf life.

Most other vegetables purchased fresh in season should at other times be supplied frozen by dealers specializing in institutional service. They will put up such goods in 1- to 5-pound packages with cuts and sizes most adaptable to commercial use. The price cycle for frozen vegetables does not fluctuate as widely as other types of merchandise, usually remaining at a reasonably static level from one packing period to the other.

The buyer simply can not avoid paying current market prices for highly perishable merchandise like lettuce, tomatoes, green peppers, cucumbers, green onions, or other such items. When prices are high, management may determine to effect savings by eliminating certain of these items from the menu, or by making substitutions where possible. For example, romaine lettuce may be used for bulk salads, since it has fewer price fluctuations and is in more general year-round supply.

Just as in the case of other wholesale merchants, produce purveyors have a delivery cost problem. With this in mind, it is imperative that smaller institutions desiring to get the most for their money from the wholesaler consolidate orders whenever possible. Although many wholesalers will have a $25 minimum average for orders, due to the perishable nature of their products, most will deliver smaller amounts providing that subsequent orders compensate for the costs involved.

The price differential between wholesale and retail produce is approximately 20 percent, which makes wholesale buying attractive to the smaller organizations. Quality levels and standards at the wholesale level will also be more flexible, allowing the buyer considerable latitude in choosing the grades or merchandise best suited to his particular needs.

12.

Buying Poultry

Forecast purchasing, though easily arranged, is not generally used in buying chickens. The general market condition is such that a constant abundant supply of all sizes and classes of birds prevails at a relatively static price. Location buying by contract does, however, have value if a quantity of birds are steadily required. The heavy poultry raising areas of the southern states as well as California have spot prices at the growers level which can benefit the buyer even after adding shipping charges. Contracts with the growers for direct shipment eliminates both the distributor and the wholesaler. Once arrangements are made the birds are shipped in ice packs since the producers rarely have means of volume freezing. Regardless of the source, ice-pack birds sell for somewhat less than frozen birds and are preferred since they can be treated as fresh poultry. The cost of freezing and packaging varies from $.02 to $.05 per pound, which creates a selling price of from 10 to 20 percent above those packed in ice.

Chickens are always shipped fully dressed with the giblets wrapped separately.

Ice-packed birds keep well and withstand shipping conditions without deterioration. Continued icing after they are received ensures freshness for from 1 to 3 weeks if the crates are refrigerated at temperatures between 34 and 42 degrees. Giblets are best removed immediately and frozen.

The savings created by buying direct from the grower can be estimated at between 10 and 15 percent. An extreme example in direct buying can be cited in the case of one of the major fast food franchise outlets specializing in fried chicken which reported buying 1¾ to 2¼ pound friers at $.17 per pound at a time when the wholesale market held to a steady $.27.

Turkeys and ducks are more seasonal in demand and are almost always purchased from wholesalers. They are almost never contracted for as the price remains stabilized except at holiday periods and then the supply is abundant. Rock Cornish game hens are a specialty item only produced for specified wholesale outlets. They, too, are always available at a fairly static cost.

Grading

All poultry is checked by the United States Department of Agriculture to assure that birds reaching the market are of edible quality and are free from contamination. Though a set of grades exists for poultry, it is not mandatory and is rarely used except in a small segment of interstate trading and in specified instances where the buyer will insist on grading and pay for the difference in cost. This makes it important for the buyer to be familiar with market practices and to be able to specify, select, and purchase according to the exact needs of the organization.

Quality birds of all kinds will have a smooth, tender skin. The breast bone will be tender to the touch and flexible. Size in itself is not a factor since some breeds are smaller at a given age than others.

For buying poultry, the following specifications will prevail in the majority of birds reaching the wholesale market:

Chicken

Method of supply: All birds will be fully dressed and eviscerated if purchased whole body and will be either fresh, frozen, or ice-packed. Giblets will be packaged and included in the weight of the bird when delivered. Cut up pieces are available frozen and packaged without giblets.

Meat yield: The cooked meat yield of all size birds will be 42 percent of the body weight.

Sizes: Broilers are sold 1½ pounds to 2½ pounds, friers 2½ pounds to 3½ pounds, roasters 3 to 6 pounds, stewing hens or cocks 3 to 6 pounds.

Size variations: In each type of bird the size variation will have a tolerance of ¼ pound above or below the size specified when ordered.

Portioned pieces: Frozen and portioned breasts will be supplied in graded sizes exactly as ordered according to available supply. Other individual pieces will be supplied only by random weight. Portioned pieces are usually only available frozen if a large quantity of individual pieces is ordered.

Turkey

Method of supply: All birds will be fully dressed and eviscerated and will be available either fresh or frozen in peak periods of supply or frozen in slow market periods. Giblets will be packaged and included in the weight of the bird when delivered.

Meat yield: The cooked meat yield will range from 48 to 53 percent of the raw body weight, increasing from the lower figure as the size of the bird increases.

Sizes: The size range runs from 12 pounds to 32 pounds for whole dressed and eviscerated birds in general supply in the market.

Size variations: The size tolerance for turkeys is 2 pounds, with this tolerance specified as 12 to 14 pounds, 24 to 26 pounds, etc. Any size falling within the range of the tolerance will be considered "as ordered."

Portioned pieces: The market for portioned turkey pieces is not substantial. Breasts are sometime available in specified sizes with legs and wings packaged only by random weight.

Duck

Young ducks classified as Peking or Long Island are available frozen in sizes from 3 to 4½ pounds with a tolerance of ¼ pound in the weight specified. The cooked meat yield is 20 percent of the raw body weight.

13.

Buying Preportioned, Precooked or Ready-to-Cook Foods

The decision to buy preportioned items for the institution kitchen should be governed by whether a significant food-cost savings can be achieved, whether labor costs can be cut, whether overall efficiency can be improved, and whether quality standards can be maintained.

In making an evaluation the most frequent problem for inplant production which arises will have to do with the skills available and how the labor costs affect the cost of the end product. Also to be considered is whether the additional work will be a burden to the kitchen and whether added labor will be required to maintain the work load. If a kitchen staff is already working at an efficient capacity the additional work of preparing items available preportioned and ready to use could disrupt the entire production schedule.

Beyond the labor factor, consideration must also be given to the expertise of processors who will have a revenue producing use for all trim resulting from production. The specialists will have little or no waste and can pass such economies forward in their selling price while in the institution the trim resulting from processing might end up as waste or in a stock pot where the value is negligible with the result being that costs are escalated unnecessarily.

After considering costs the quality standards should be evaluated by ascertaining whether in such items as veal, pork, or beef cutlets the purchased product has not been impregnated with added fats and liquids which will lower the taste potentials and create a hidden waste by shrinkage when cooked. Although the Food and Drug Administration regulations set maximums of 10 percent water in frankfurters or cold meats, 8 percent in poultry products, and 20 percent in fresh meat products, the producer may add more providing the label indicates the addition. Ground meat products of all kinds are frequent violators of these guidelines, however, since in the grinding process the processor feeds a steady flow of crushed ice into the grinder to keep the meat and the cutting blades cold so the meat will be sharply cut instead of crushed as it passes through the machine. This need for controlling temperatures increases the bulk of the meat and its weight since the water becomes an integral part of the product. If the processor adds ice beyond that actually needed to the point where he creates an excess of 20 percent of moisture content in the meat he immediately begins to sell water for the same price as the meat. It is possible to stay within the bounds of the prescribed moisture content of the meat while adding ice, and most reliable purveyors will restrict their operation accordingly.

Fats are injected into tenderized cutlets by adding material which has been frozen and finely ground, sprinkling it evenly over the meat as it passes through the blades of the tenderizing mechanism. Cod fat is often used for this purpose and in its favor it does add flavor although it will be dissipated during the cooking process and cause undue shrinkage.

A simple weight-taste test can be made by comparing products produced in the kitchen with those purchased. The shrinkage can be compared if each product is weighed before and after cooking. The palatability standard will depend upon the opinion of those making the taste test. All costs and tastes being equal, the inplant product will always have an ephemeral or evasive cost due to all the factors involved in its production while the purchased product will have an exact cost. Another factor to be considered is that of inventory control. Where purchases are made in a known quantity a known number of servings can be expected against an approximate number of portions which will be created in the kitchen from a bulk of material. Most organizations find that where quality and cost per portion between the two processes are closely comparable that the advantages exist in the use of preportioned products.

The use of precooked canned and frozen foods also demands a certain amount of investigation if costs and quality standards are to be maintained. The Food and Drug Administration and the food industry have for some years been cooperating in a move to increase the use of nutritional labeling for such products. Some labels are now standardized to show the relative protein, vitamins, minerals, fats, and carbohydrates of the contents. While this is a useful aid for dietary purposes, it does not establish the percentage of each basic food in the preparation.

The buyer should be informed not only about the nutritional value of the product but more importantly about the percentage of the protein values of milk, meat, poultry, fish, and eggs. In some cases frozen raw products will be extended with such items as water, starch, sugar, fat, or other fillers not easily detected. These fillers are often used to replace meat solids.

There is no move at present to require the processor to list the actual contents of a package or can, although some of the more concerned and progressive firms packing for the food industry do provide them, for example the contents of a beef stew can would be listed as follows:

Sauce (water, beef extracts, flour,
        paste, salt, onion powder,
        coloring, and pepper)   60 percent
Lean beef   25 percent
Potatoes   10 percent
Carrots   5 percent

This type of labeling should be sought out by the buyer so that comparative portion cost can be established against similar products made in the institutional kitchen. When the percentage of ingredients is unknown the actual meat contents in such a can or package may be minimal, with the bulk being inexpensive fillers.

Canned or processed foods produced for retail rarely list the percentages of ingredients or offer clearly definitive labeling to describe the product's composition. Thus the buyer should deal with purveyors who deal only with restaurants or institutions. Almost all such purveyors will gladly discuss portion costing and the relative values of the products they distribute.

Ready-to-cook foods are available in various forms though they are generally supplied only in a frozen condition. Some require only warming though most must be fully cooked. The major interests of the institution is toward ready-prepared entrees, breaded raw cutlets, shrimp and other seafoods, and ready-to-bake bakery products some of which are shown in Figure 14.

Frozen, mixed-ingredient entrees supplied in bulk and packed in oven-ready transfer pans which fit into warming table insets may appear simple and foolproof with the need to follow oven temperature and time of cooking being the only concern. Such simplicity is rarely the case, however. Few combinations of foods cook to the proper consistency and stages of doneness at the same temperature and in the

Fig. 14. *Oven-ready and ready-to-eat bakery products, and ready-to-cook entrees and canned foods.*

same exact amount of time. This is one of the major faults found in ready-to-cook mixtures. If meats are cooked to the proper state, vegetables sometimes become over cooked and fragmented, and the sauces break and become thin and watery with a lack of flavor. If the vegetables are cooked to the exact proper state the meats may be too rare and tough. If the sauce is given top consideration none of the other ingredients will be properly cooked. A competent cook can, however, cope with the sauce problem by adding roux to restore its consistency and if necessary add seasonings to revive its flavor.

These problems are a continuing situation because the processor will need to use foods having natural changes of quality from time to time, causing each product to vary from its predecessor. An understanding of this is found in almost all cooking procedures where cooking times vary from day to day even though the ingredients do not. If these products are to be used, cooking techniques will be required beyond those of cooking at a given temperature for a given amount of time.

Convenience is a marginal factor favorable to this type of product. Without exception the portion cost will equal or far exceed those of similar items prepared in the institutional kitchen. They will lack the qualities of personally prepared food in the matters of taste and texture since most have been created by food engineers rather than culinary experts.

Just as in the case of canned foods, labeling is important and only those products having clearly definitive labels should be considered.

Ready-to-cook raw cutlets, shrimp, and other seafood items also require investigation before they are considered for use. In packaging, the label will rarely state the net weight of the meats involved. When it is given it may indicate that a 4-ounce cutlet may have as much as 25 percent breading material, making the actual net weight of the meat only 3 ounces. This also applies to seafoods such as patties, fish sticks, or breaded fillets of all kinds. Shrimp are often coated with a puff breading containing leaveners to create the illusion of size after they are cooked. If these flaws are eliminated and a careful selection made from available products which do not exaggerate size by over-breading, good to excellent results can be achieved by using this type of merchandise. Most are processed at the time of low cycles in the cost scale and are sold in the market on a competitive basis.

Frozen ready-to-bake bakery products are usually superior to inplant products and they are foolproof if baking temperatures and times are closely followed. The cost factor is lower than inplant products because of volume production and competitive market conditions. Varieties are endless for institutional purposes.

Uncooked frozen foods offer an economical source for many bread, pie, and pastry items as well as bulk doughs. Puff paste is traditionally packed in either 30 pound bricks or 6/5 pound bricks per case and Danish dough in 22 pound bricks. Individual Danish pastries, ready formed, are generally packed 72 to the carton. Pie shells are available in 3 inch (tart size), 4½ inch (pot pie size), and 8, 9, or 10 inch standard pie sizes, usually packed 24 or 48 pieces per carton. Unformed pie sheets are available in the same diameters, packed 24 pieces per carton. Thaw and bake breads come in 6 ounce demi-loaf size or regular 1 pound size. Parkerhouse rolls are available in cases of either 120 or 240 pieces.

Brown and serve rolls come in many varieties, costing only slightly more than frozen raw rolls. The difference in cost is sometimes accounted for in the convenience of these products since they may be put in the oven in a frozen condition and by their being partially baked, they will be ready to serve when properly browned. Some purveyors offer demi-loaf bread or small size French or Italian sour dough bread in a brown and serve product that is also satisfactory. Packaging varies in different localities. These products are generally sold by frozen food vendors and not wholesale bakers.

14.

Establishing a Menu Selling Price

Once management has determined what the food portions and their cost will be, sound merchandising principles require that stable and reasonable prices be established. Prices must, of course, coincide with the price structure of the establishment and beyond that, must allow for a just and reasonable profit. If a balanced profit margin is to be maintained, all menu items will have to maintain the same cost to sales ratio. It has long been established in low budget cookery that to lower the price of a costly item to adjust it to the balance of the low cost menu or to accommodate the customer is a costly mistake. If this policy is practiced, the low cost items will be forced to carry the losses created by the narrowed profit margin of the high cost items.

Assuming that a low cost item has been selected and the food prepared in an amount that will produce 100 portions at a total cost of $24, the food cost will be 24 cents per portion. If a full meal is to be served, side dishes such as vegetables, potatoes, bread and butter will add on the average approximately 25 percent to the cost of the entree. The plate cost will then be $.30.

If employee feeding is added to food cost instead of to payroll cost, include an allowance of between 3 and 5 percent of the overall food cost. An additional 1 percent for waste occurring after preparation should also be figured in. Taking the higher percentage of employee feeding cost along with the percentage of waste, the plate cost now rises to $.36.

Before a stable allowance for total food cost can be determined, other more static expenses must be taken into account. In a full service restaurant operating under a union labor contract, the average payroll cost includes Social Security, unemployment compensation insurance, industrial accident insurance, and health and welfare benefits. These will average between 35 percent to 37 percent of the incoming dollar. After these expenses must come the overhead operating expenses which will take another 25 percent of the incoming dollar on the average. Thus, 62 percent of the incoming dollar has been consumed (.37 + .25). No allowance has been made as yet for a profit margin. A realistic profit figure is 12 percent of the gross, which added to payroll and overhead, accounts for $.74 of each dollar of income, leaving a maximum of $.26 to cover the cost of the food served.

To cover these costs, food must be sold for about 4 times its direct preparation cost. In other words, food cost should be approximately 25 percent of menu price. Thus, the $.36 plate should be sold for a minimum of $1.44. In general practice the selling price would be rounded off to $1.50 to cover contingencies.

In fast food operations and/or highly competitive situations where labor and overhead expenses are reduced, menu price may be cut back to 2½ times cost (40 percent) or 3 times cost (33-1/3 percent), depending on how much of each incoming dollar is consumed by fixed costs.

Prudent management of pricing can be achieved only by diligent application of systematic, standardized methods, taking care that there is always a slight margin in management's favor for coping with losses created by carelessness in preparation and service. If the kitchen is operating efficiently, and there are still leaks which cause an unaccountable escalation in projected food costs, a check at the service end of the operation is called for. Service personnel may be charging incorrectly, either failing to list correct menu prices or neglecting to add in items such as salads, desserts, or beverages. These, individually, are minor matters to be sure. If left uncontrolled, however, they will substantially reduce the profit margin.

15.

The Rotating Menu Program

A rotating menu program whereby a series of menus are rotated from day to day, usually for the period of a week, has a number of definite advantages. Primarily such a program stabilizes production in a systematic manner and facilitates buying in advance for a price advantage either by contract methods or forecast marketing. Without such a program buying in advance or making projections for needs becomes difficult. Where it is known that an article of food is to be used regularly on a particular day, delivery schedules can be arranged with purveyors which eliminates haphazard purchasing which can then create stock shortages or inventory surpluses.

To prevent monotony in a repeatedly used menu or bored patrons from a constant and unsystematic one, Figure 15 shows a daily menu advertisement which outlines how specials can be arranged on a static basic menu in a rotating manner. The first two items of the menu were specials of the day and prepared for that day only. The items vary in type from the balance of the menu made up from regular prepared-to-order menu listings. Each day of the week the two specials differ for that day. In event of leftovers on any day, the items can be used on subsequent days or for luncheons by placing them on a menu attached flyer until they are sold. Frequently an audience is created when patrons become familiar with the day a favored item will be offered.

By the kitchen having a regular program, complementary items such as sauces, gravies, and dressings can be made at one time to sufficiently carry through the week. An example could be in white cream gravy used on Mondays as an underliner for breaded veal cutlets. If the

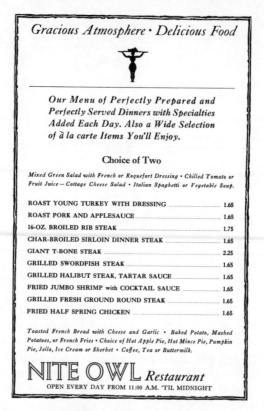

Gracious Atmosphere · Delicious Food

Our Menu of Perfectly Prepared and Perfectly Served Dinners with Specialties Added Each Day. Also a Wide Selection of à la carte Items You'll Enjoy.

Choice of Two

Mixed Green Salad with French or Roquefort Dressing · Chilled Tomato or Fruit Juice — Cottage Cheese Salad · Italian Spaghetti or Vegetable Soup.

ROAST YOUNG TURKEY WITH DRESSING	1.65
ROAST PORK AND APPLESAUCE	1.65
16-OZ. BROILED RIB STEAK	1.75
CHAR-BROILED SIRLOIN DINNER STEAK	1.65
GIANT T-BONE STEAK	2.25
GRILLED SWORDFISH STEAK	1.65
GRILLED HALIBUT STEAK, TARTAR SAUCE	1.65
FRIED JUMBO SHRIMP with COCKTAIL SAUCE	1.65
GRILLED FRESH GROUND ROUND STEAK	1.65
FRIED HALF SPRING CHICKEN	1.65

Toasted French Bread with Cheese and Garlic · Baked Potato, Mashed Potatoes, or French Fries · Choice of Hot Apple Pie, Hot Mince Pie, Pumpkin Pie, Jello, Ice Cream or Sherbet · Coffee, Tea or Buttermilk.

NITE OWL *Restaurant*
OPEN EVERY DAY FROM 11:00 A.M. 'TIL MIDNIGHT

Fig. 15. *A typical daily menu in an inexpensive restaurant.*

kitchen is aware that chicken croquettes, which also calls for an underliner, are to be served on Wednesday, and macaroni and cheese, which needs the white sauce for a stabilizer, on Friday, then sufficient quantities can be made in one operation.

In institutions other than restaurants and cafeterias where the preparation techniques of the staff will be less than that of professional cooks, repetitive production of specific items will improve work aptitudes markedly. The production program will require less and less supervision and mistakes will become fewer as the process becomes standardized.

In a restaurant where a large variety of foods are required for each day the buying can be adjusted to meet demand. The institution, by its basic method of operation, will require fewer numbers of food items although the overall quantities used may be equal or larger. By arriving at a set standard of needs for each week savings can be made in buying because of the interest the larger bulk of goods will create among purveyors. While a restaurant might produce 50 orders of a prepared item, a medium sized institutional operation will produce from 100 to 300 orders of a similar product and will need greater amounts of bulk ingredients. This creates an ideal atmosphere for forecast or contract buying.

Important to administration is that decisions are minimized in the production and buying program. An entire year of planning can be set forth in one session and carried forward from year to year. To be able to foresee needs at any point of the operation the only requirement for future operation will be to add to or subtract from the buying or production schedule to meet an unusual happening. Growth rates can be estimated and adjusted from time to time and the program updated to fit ongoing projections. Open market purchasing can be reduced to incidental items and instinct buying for items not actually needed eliminated.

The Karabian Investment Company, operators of board and care half-way houses under contract with the state of California found a solution in supplying the kitchens of their network operations without the need for a commissary by setting up a schedule of two rotating menus, alternating between them after one week of use. They prepare a controlled buying schedule for each menu, listing every item needed for producing the foods to be served. Operating on the premise that management at the point of need will be minimal, the buying is done at their main office with delivery schedules set up for each supplying purveyor. The local manager has the authority to make only restricted open market purchases for incidental needs on a daily basis with inventories at each point held to current needs. The operation is based on a full occupancy for each of the differing sized units they operate, which vary from 50 to 300 semipermanent occupants.

The food prepared in each unit is based on two items in each category for three different types of feeding. Under supervision of a dietitian, who also dispenses necessary medications prescribed by medical authorities, the feeding is personalized by the color of an identification card each person must present. The categories are diet oriented meals: bland meals where seasonings are controlled and regular meals where no controls exist.

Without a systematized series of rotating menus the remote management control policy would be inoperable and economically unsound. Stringent controls at every step are needed because funding for the program allows only for the barest minimum of localized supervision with most of the kitchen and cafeteria work being done by those housed in the establishments. This new concept of caring for those who would otherwise be in state hospitals, minimal security mental institutions, or rehabilitation centers is one that is gaining rapid popularity.

Eighteen states are now beginning the same type of program. The states, which previously collected taxes for maintaining such persons in institutions, return to the local authorities $4,000.00 per year for each person and that money is then turned back to the community for arranging their care and providing food and lodging. The food stipulations are that three meals comparable to restaurant standards must be served each person three times daily. The medication program is separately endowed and supervised. The program covers mobile adults known as the walking wounded who are capable of caring for themselves if food and housing is provided.

By use of a menu control system where waste and mistakes in buying can be eliminated, the operating firm can work within the restrictive funding available and show a profit. The Karabian Company caters to 30,000 persons on a semipermanent basis. The illustration here is that an inexperienced food operator by adhering to a systematic operation can profitably feed and house a large number of persons. There are no provisions for increasing the funding to meet food cost problems which means that the operator will be forced to continue an efficient operation.

The rotating menu program may be flexible. The general guideline necessary to one type of operation also applies to any other. The basic goal is to arrive at a standard kitchen production schedule and buying program which fits a specific period of time. Having both a predetermined work schedule and buying schedule increases the efficiency of kitchen production and purchasing. It creates economies by determining exact amounts of merchandise needed for production, and the taste, texture, and palatability of the product produced is improved as the kitchen techniques become improved. The process allows for an assembly line type of receipt of merchandise to fit the production of menu items which can also proceed in the same precise manner. When the menu is rotated the program needs only slight modifications to replace one item with another. As was illustrated in Figure 15, the basic total production schedule for a restaurant remains static with only incidental listings being changed. This also applies to cafeterias offering the usual menu augmented by specific specials for each succeeding day. Institutions may need to make more drastic changes; creating entirely new menus for each specified period of time but always returning to the cycle of repeating previous menus in a programmed rotation. This prevents fragmentation in the buying schedules and maintains productivity improvements in the kitchen which have been gained by repetitive preparation of a particular food item.

16.

Basic
Equipment Requirements

For volume food production, the essence of low-budget cookery, certain basic equipment is vital. In the commercial restaurant the preparation kitchen is usually a separate entity, operating independently of the service kitchen where foods are dispensed and short orders prepared. The amount of equipment needed for the preparation kitchen will vary according to the volume of food to be produced. The general outline of equipment needs will be stable, however, and will adapt to modification if the volume is expanded. Figures 16, 17, and 18 illustrate various types of kitchen equipment.

Ample work space is a must, and work tables should be used as extensively as space will allow. These should be arranged to eliminate unnecessary walking by placing them close to all preparation equipment. Standard work tables are available in many lengths and widths, making adaptation and selection simple.

For preparing soups, stews, or fricassees, for cooking large amounts of vegetables or making soup stocks, stationary jacketed cooking kettles are best. The medium size installation should have at least two such cookers of 10-gallon capacity or greater. This allows for the simultaneous preparation of two masses of stews or similar foods or for one entree to be in progress while a quantity of soup is also being prepared. Although large stock pots serve the same purpose, the process is not as efficient nor the results as good. The stationary jacketed kettle prevents burning or scorching and is easily emptied by large drain valves

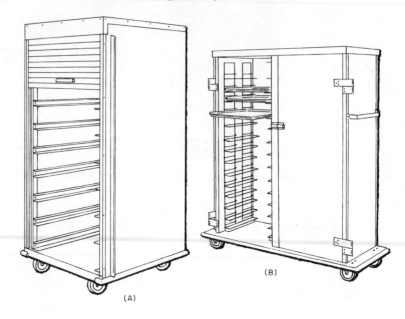

(A)

(B)

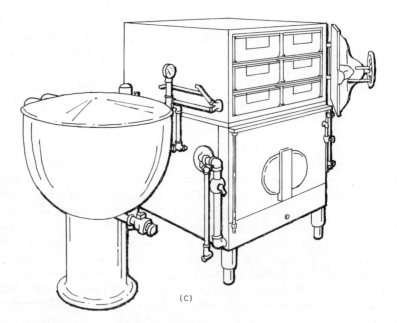

(C)

Fig. 16. *(A) Roller door cart*
(B) Insulated food moving cabinet
(C) Jacketed kettle combined with steamer unit

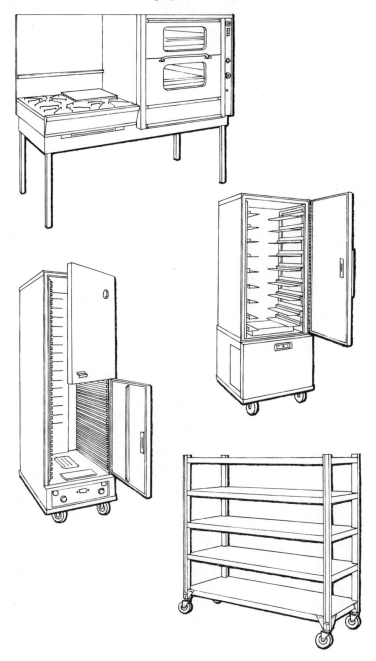

Fig. 17. *Utility hot cabinet and mobile modular units.*

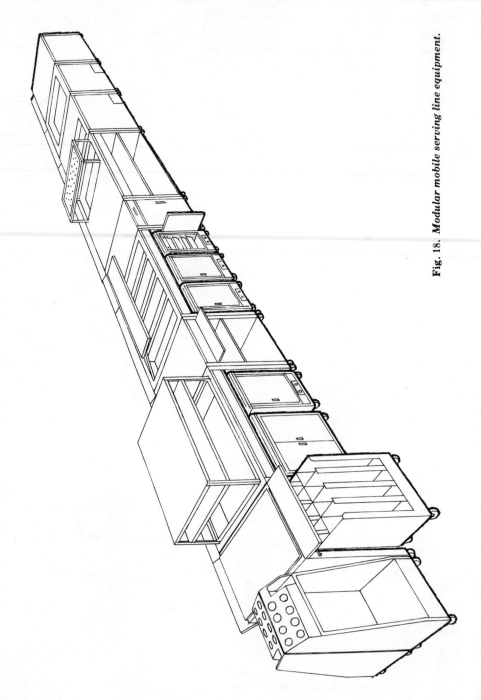

Fig. 18. *Modular mobile serving line equipment.*

at the bottom, which makes draining quick as well as safe. Such cookers are available in direct-fired gas or electric units or in steam units, where live steam is available from a central installation.

Stack ovens are essential where baking and roasting are extensive. They come in from one to four tiers. Additional tiers can be added as needs increase. Each tier can operate at a different temperature, making several cooking procedures possible at one time. The units are available for use with either gas or electricity.

Range-top cooking will require a unit with at least six open burners plus a flat grill-type area equal in size to that of the open burners. (Such ranges also have ovens which can be used to augment tier ovens at peak production periods.) Burners should be spaced to allow for a number of large pots without crowding. The flat grill-type area can be used for either slow simmering or cooking.

Steamers for rapid cooking can add efficiency to any kitchen, regardless of size. Steamers come in both free-venting and pressure types. The former require somewhat more time for cooking; the latter cook very rapidly under controlled, adjustable pressures. Commercial pressure cookers have extensive safety features and alarm systems which can be time set. Both types of steamers are available in electric or gas models; still another style can be hooked into live steam.

A commercial power mixer is also essential. There are table mounted models of from 2- to 3-gallon capacity and 5- to 10-gallon floor mounted models. Some models have attachments for grinding and food chopping.

If the food service area is not located near the preparation kitchen, transportation equipment for conveying hot foods or large masses of foods is important. This equipment not only speeds up food flow from the kitchen to the warming or serving tables but also increases safety. The cost of one serious accident resulting from handling hot foods can be far more than the cost of preventive equipment. Standard food movers are available in numerous sizes and arrangements, but equipment distributors will also custom manufacture equipment to fit special needs and at a relatively low additional cost.

For accurate portion control a good portioning scale is indispensable. Scales especially designed for restaurant use are best. Such scales have a quick reflex which allows for speedy portioning. They also feature an over-and-under indicator which clearly shows whether too much or too little has been placed on the weighing platform. A sensitive, reliable portioning scale costs below $100.

Refrigeration equipment should always be as extensive as room size and budget permit. Smaller units can function with reach-in boxes providing they are spacious enough for perishable foods needed from day to day and for holding extra supplies for holidays or week-ends. Larger units should have not only convenient reach-in refrigerators but also a walk-in type for storing large amounts of perishables. Such units should be capable of maintaining a constant temperature of above 32 degrees and below 45 degrees; reach-in models should hold to temperatures of below 40 degrees and above 32 degrees.

Freezer units should have a capacity matching exactly the amount of frozen merchandise the organization will use. Chest type units where goods can be stored in full view are the most practical. Freezers in daily use for short-term storage should be capable of maintaining a temperature of between zero and 5 degrees. Storage units where merchandise is to be kept for a prolonged period should be capable of holding a constant sub-zero temperature.

Kitchen Layouts

Kitchen layouts may vary to suit production needs. A prime consideration in all arrangements should be to organize the working area to prevent unnecessary steps or motions. Working aisles should provide only enough space for turning from one line of equipment to the other without having to take steps. For a compact layout, aisles should measure between 36 and 40 inches and all equipment should be placed side by side without unnecessary space in between. All work tables and the working level of equipment should be approximately waist-high to give the best working posture for efficiency and ease of operation.

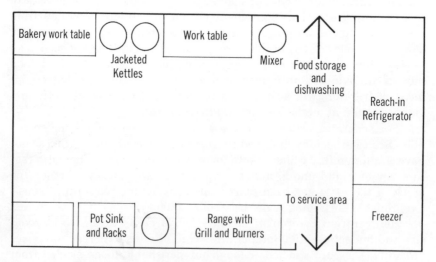

Fig. 19. *Standard kitchen layout without service facilities.*

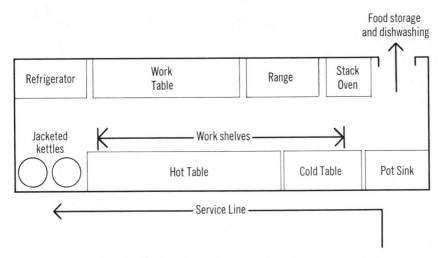

Fig. 20. *Standard cafeteria kitchen floor plan with service facilities.*

The diagram in Figure 19 is a standard kitchen layout for a preparation kitchen which would function equally well in a restaurant, cafeteria, or institution. There is no provision in this plan for the kitchen having any part in the eventual serving of prepared foods. Item A can be either a slicer or grinder.

Figure 20 illustrates a standard cafeteria kitchen floor plan where the preparation staff can participate in the service function. In this plan dish storage can be optional. They may be held on shelves be-

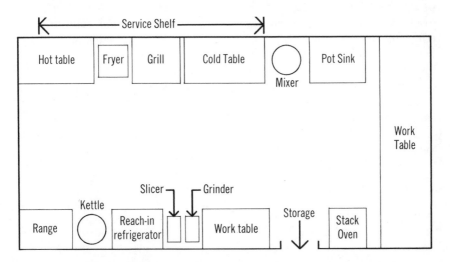

Fig. 21. *Kitchen layout for restaurant, including preparation and service facilities.*

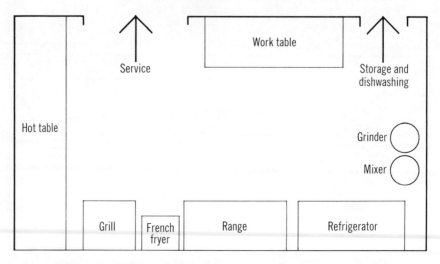

Fig. 22. *Small functional kitchen with capacity to prepare and serve bulk and short order meals.*

neath the warming and cold tables or on shelving over the serving tables. In commercial installations catering to the public a glass sneeze-shield may be a requirement in some areas to prevent the public from coming in contact with the food.

A combination preparation and service kitchen for restaurant operation is illustrated in Figure 21. This kitchen layout is effective for producing bulk products, bakery products, and short orders for a comprehensive operation. It can operate to produce a good volume with two cooks and a cook's helper or its productivity can be expanded to a very heavy production schedule by adding additional workers.

A small, functional kitchen in which one cook with the aid of a combination utility worker-dishwasher can both prepare and serve a substantial volume of food is illustrated in Figure 22. This kitchen would be equally efficient for a small dinner house, general restaurant, or institutional cafeteria type operation where the display of food is not necessary. It will function for producing bulk foods and short orders or a combination of both.

17.

Food Preparation Personnel

An economy oriented food program directs its food preparation system toward providing the largest possible number of servings with the greatest possible ease and efficiency of production. To achieve this goal, the organization must utilize personnel without comprehensive culinary experience, and the volume feeding operation does not hire a chef, or baker, or other high-priced specialists. This places the burden of creative supervision squarely on the kitchen manager, who will direct less experienced employees. Essential for the volume preparation kitchen are personnel who are adaptable and flexible in their work attitudes. As an example of the need for adaptability among employees, the various duties for one day's operation can be used. In a commercial restaurant kitchen generating foods for a daily volume of between $500 and $900 with the actual serving performed by others, the operation would require one qualified journeyman cook, one experienced cook's helper and one general kitchen worker. These three would be required to produce the following typical basic foods over and beyond any bulk short-order items the menu might list:

3 luncheon entrees
1 luncheon soup
2 salads sufficient for the day's operation
3 salad dressings, usually prepared in bulk
sufficient mashed potatoes for luncheon
sufficient vegetables for luncheon
hot rolls or breads for luncheon

plate garnishes
luncheon desserts
sauces or gravies for the day's operation
2 hot dinner entrees
baked or other potatoes for dinner
meat cutting for both meal and short-order needs
dinner breads
dinner soups
dinner vegetables
dinner desserts.

Figures from the U.S. Department of Labor indicate that between 25 and 30 percent of the nation's restaurants operate under labor conditions imposed by various branches of the Culinary Workers Union of the American Federation of Labor. Under the terms of such labor agreements, which by their widespread use set a general pattern, the duties of food preparation fall into a category covered by craftsmen of one classification or another. This spectrum of workers includes chefs, second cooks, broilermen, fry cooks, pantrymen, cook's helpers, and miscellaneous workers, with pay scales varying from category to category. Because no distinct guidelines exist, any craftsman can be assigned duties generally defined as institutional cooking which that person is capable of performing.

In using qualified craftsmen, regardless of the type of operation, personnel productivity and capability should be more or less assured, leaving for management the fairly simple determination of how many workers are required to satisfy food production needs. Each organization will have varying schedules of needs, with the list expanding where there is a large volume of short-order items and diminishing where short-order volume is limited. Staff size should be based on the number of functions or procedures that must be in progress simultaneously to meet time schedules.

Labor policies of institutions operating under any of the various governmental agencies vary from those of commercial restaurants or institutions. Usually, only key supervisory personnel are provided, most often through an established Civil Service Commission system which prescribes the exact job qualifications to be applied. They then proceed to fill related positions with such people as trustees in detention units or miscellaneous workers in other branches of food production programs. The reasoning here is that most of the food prepared is based on simple formulas. Moreover, there are fewer production procedures, since most foods are prepared in large uniform quantities. Unskilled workers with adequate supervision are therefore able to produce acceptable end products. The details of operating the institutional kitchen will be minimal in comparison to those of the commercial kitchen serving an equal number of people.

Hospital kitchens in medium size operations are usually under the direction of a dietitian who acts as kitchen manager and supervisor and who is responsible for the production program. These dietitians execute all planning, menu preparation, scheduling, and food estimations. The staff compares with that of a medium size restaurant, with a journeyman cook assisted by cook's helpers or miscellaneous workers trained in kitchen procedures. Kitchen personnel for hospitals should be those who can follow directions, since the stress is on nutritional balance as opposed to taste and presentation.

Small institutions such as rest homes for the aged, convalescent homes, boarding schools, or other relatively small feeding units will rarely have the financial means to enable them to staff their kitchens with professionals. These organizations will usually need to resort to hiring semiretired cooks, trained cook's helpers, or persons with sufficient talent to handle food production under the direct supervision of a qualified manager.

School feeding programs with on-premises food preparation, as opposed to commissary service, involve simple procedures. Most often the master program is outlined by a qualified dietitian, with the actual preparation carried out by either volunteer workers or persons with only basic skills. Workers will need minimum training to prepare portions and balances such as those outlined in the Type A Feeding Program described in chapter 4. Practically all foods are supplied in ready-to-warm or ready-to-serve condition; almost never is any cooking involved beyond thawing frozen or highly refrigerated goods and then only heating and portioning. Most programs do involve sandwich making but in each case the meats are supplied ready to use with stipulated amounts of spreads or garnishes.

18.

An Easy-to-Keep
Daily Check on
Food Costs

After any system has been organized and is functioning, checks and double checks become a necessary corollary to the system. Although the monthly profit and loss statement or the monthly budget balance sheet constitutes an ongoing report of the system's success or failure, these reports are made only after the fact. Furthermore, when losses have occurred, these forms do not always pinpoint the source. The most essential function of management is therefore to assure that such reports turn out favorably and that leaks and losses are not occurring during the interim operating period.

To keep a constant vigil on daily expenditures, a simple and workable daily check sheet on goods received should be instituted. This will exert control on such divergencies as overbuying, overproducing, waste, kitchen malfunctions in preparation, pilferage, and delivery shortages. The check sheet makes possible the immediate detection of loss before it can reach major proportions.

To set up a functional yet informal daily cost analysis, use a pad with twenty or more columns to the page. Head each column with a regularly ordered item such as: Hamburger, Boneless Chuck, Chicken, Shrimp, Fish Fillets, Potatoes, Lettuce, Carrots, Peas, Green Beans, etc.

For a cafeteria operation in a commercial establishment or an institution where serving hours are restricted, Figure 23 illustrates a work schedule where the same sized crew could both prepare and serve foods produced in the system outlined in the following chart but in lesser quantities and without preparing short-order needs for the service kitchen.

A typical daily production schedule is outlined in Figure 24. This schedule could be applicable to any type operation where the preparation staff does not participate in the serving of the foods prepared.

The number of individual items may seem awesome at first, but the more comprehensive the breakdown, the more effective will be the report. Under each heading, list the quantity on hand when the report is started, ideally in conjunction with the formal monthly inventory. Each day the deliveries are entered in the proper column. Although either the quantity or the dollar volume will make the report functional, a more informative analysis can be made if both figures are entered. This report has no connection with formal bookkeeping procedures and has no relation with how the goods are paid for or by what method. It concerns only all goods received, no matter the origin of the order or its connection with permanent records.

One feature which will make the report more readily available for comparison will be a weekly summary of receipts. As time goes on this will result in a clear picture of merchandise ordered and either consumed or in storage.

During the first month of record keeping it will be necessary to make estimates of money spent and/or merchandise received as they

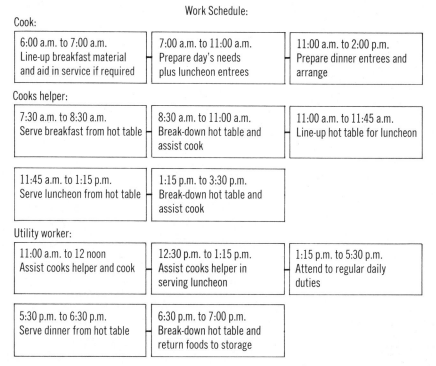

Work Schedule:

Cook:

| 6:00 a.m. to 7:00 a.m. Line-up breakfast material and aid in service if required | 7:00 a.m. to 11:00 a.m. Prepare day's needs plus luncheon entrees | 11:00 a.m. to 2:00 p.m. Prepare dinner entrees and arrange |

Cooks helper:

| 7:30 a.m. to 8:30 a.m. Serve breakfast from hot table | 8:30 a.m. to 11:00 a.m. Break-down hot table and assist cook | 11:00 a.m. to 11:45 a.m. Line-up hot table for luncheon |

| 11:45 a.m. to 1:15 p.m. Serve luncheon from hot table | 1:15 p.m. to 3:30 p.m. Break-down hot table and assist cook |

Utility worker:

| 11:00 a.m. to 12 noon Assist cooks helper and cook | 12:30 p.m. to 1:15 p.m. Assist cooks helper in serving luncheon | 1:15 p.m. to 5:30 p.m. Attend to regular daily duties |

| 5:30 p.m. to 6:30 p.m. Serve dinner from hot table | 6:30 p.m. to 7:00 p.m. Break-down hot table and return foods to storage |

Fig. 23. *Food preparation staff who also double as service personnel.*

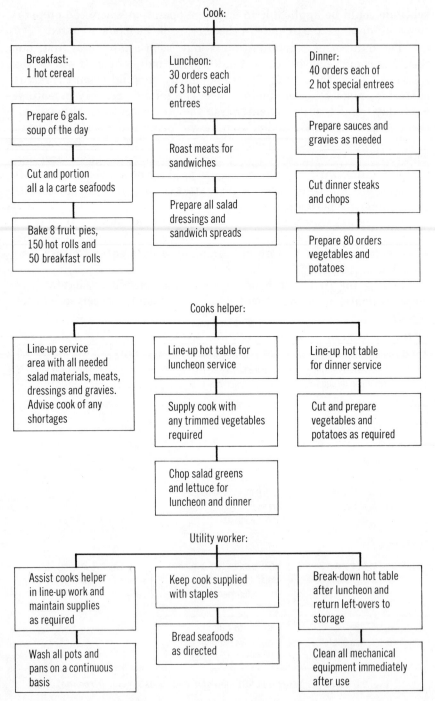

Fig. 24. *Food preparation staff without responsibility for serving food.*

relate to the dollar percentage cost projected for that month. Then at the close of the month it will be necessary to make a comparison with the closing inventory figure for the period. That new inventory is used to head the following month's report. After a few months, a quick comparison can be made with previous periods. Should there be an increase in consumption of any individual item without a related increase in dollar volume or number of people fed, a quick check is simple. If, for instance, there has been an upsurge in the purchase of an item normally ordered in a five-day cycle without an apparent corresponding increase in daily demand, immediate investigation is necessary. This will either disclose a good reason for the increase or provide grounds for closing the loophole. When the daily check sheet becomes functional it will also serve the secondary purpose of acquainting the administration with the daily operation of the kitchen and thus lead to an understanding of some of the justifiable fluctuations in food demands and costs. This informational aspect becomes more essential as the organization expands in size and the kitchen operation becomes more diverse and further from the direct domination of the management sector.

This report, followed faithfully, provides a quick control tool for tracing misapplications or physical shortages and additionally offers a long-range charting of food consumption patterns. It at once becomes a means of communication between management and kitchen, requiring only the input of intelligence and imagination to provide a complete operational picture.

19.

Profit Losses from Hidden Causes

The Department of Commerce sets feeding establishment losses from waste at approximately 5 percent of the total food purchased and losses from contrived causes—dishonesties among employees and purveyors—at from 8 to 12 percent of the same total. These two figures become vitally important to the organization bent on controlling food costs. Both figures can be minimized or even totally eliminated through adroit kitchen management and supervision.

The largest single source of waste comes from overproduction—leftovers which either are not or can not be used at another time. The obvious solution is to avoid food formulas which result in unuseable leftovers. From that simple step follows the installation of an inventory system where unused foods can be refrigerated or frozen. When new production schedules are outlined, they can then be put back into service either as an entree or as a part of a similar dish with only a simple adjustment of the formula.

Overproduction is less controllable in the commercial restaurant than in other branches of institutional feeding since the customer demands can not always be anticipated. Nevertheless, a certain amount of trial and error will eventually establish an approximate production level which can be used as a standard. Guest checks should be analyzed to determine degrees of discrepancy between the amount produced and the actual number of servings. An unpopular entree will reveal itself readily, indicating a need to drop it entirely or produce it in lesser quantity. Normally a slow item will form a distinct sales pattern which can be used as a yardstick for production. No such item should be continued on the menu after three or four efforts. This will only result in overproduction and create an overall increase in food costs. Institutional feeding units where a known number of people will be fed should have little overproduction loss if the production schedule is closely related to the needs of the establishment.

Other waste losses come from trimming and handling raw food products. Of these, meat must be singled out because of its high cost. In general, every ounce of meat has a functional value. Proper trimming should therefore separate each type and segment produced to a particular category. Muscle meat, the lean, trimmed product, will usually constitute the primary separation. All other materials such as bones, tendons, and pieces of fat can be used in one or more types of cookery, from making soup stocks to grinding for use as flavor enhancers. Muscle meat or lean bits and pieces should not be relegated to waste merely because they are small. These pieces can be collected and frozen until there is a sufficient accumulation for an entree or for making ground meat. (The details of handling and trimming meats are covered in Part Two of this book.)

Waste in fresh produce is sometimes caused by excessive trimming if the quality is poor or if the merchandise is overpurchased and held for a prolonged period. This is especially true for leaf vegetables such as lettuce, cabbage, or greens. Produce also deteriorates rapidly without proper storage and refrigeration facilities.

Pilferage is a perenially serious threat in the institutional food operation especially if the kitchen and storage area supervision is minimal. Figures from insurance underwriter groups and the Department of Commerce indicate that one can reasonably assume that almost any employee will at one time or another resort to taking merchandise from his employer. In the kitchen, pilferage is almost always connected with expensive items such as portioned raw meats or poultry. A pre-cut steak, cutlet, or poultry portion fits conveniently in a pocket or purse or can be otherwise concealed in personal belongings.

Such petty thievery can be controlled effectively if such tempting items are stored in locked refrigerators—and if an awareness exists among employees that supervision of the storage area is a regular function of the establishment. Almost no worker will pilfer if a good chance of detection exists. Effective prevention therefore should include a regular inventory, locking of the storage area, and close supervision made known to the staff. Most workers will not be tempted if the storage area is known to be under surveillance.

The most serious potential source of loss but one which can be successfully contained or prevented is that caused by dishonest delivery people. Almost without exception, any organization which does not employ a detailed system of weighing, counting, and checking every delivery of merchandise is being cheated. Prevention of loss through short delivery or underweight delivery can be achieved by the simple process of checking every delivery made, no matter how small, with the delivery manifest. Items bought by weight must be weighed in, items bought by volume must go through a comparative check of the containers, and items bought by count must be counted.

Such checking involves not only food items but laundry or other merchandise where a miscount can exist. This protects the institution against honest mistakes as well as conscious cheating, making it a necessary function for every order received. Dishonest delivery men will avoid attempting to cheat where such a system is in effect since detection is almost certain.

Part Two

The material presented in this section is not set up as a cookbook but rather as a text for use in a training program. The methods as well as the recipes are arranged to train personnel to perform a wide and varied range of tasks. Nothing herein demands a culinary expertise not common to institutional staffs. Once mastered, these methods will be applicable to various forms of preparation, all of which have a basic and essential sameness. The variations in end products will depend upon the selection of ingredients and the choice of method best suited to their preparation. By training personnel in methods of low-budget cookery, techniques improve markedly as each recipe is repeated time and again. Anyone with basic food preparation experience can, by adhering to the text, be trained to produce foods with the correct balance of texture, taste, and visual attractiveness.

This training program can also add to productivity. By repeated use of basic recipes, kitchen personnel learn to avoid confusion and indecision, thus sharpening their productive capabilities.

20.

Methods of Meat Cookery

The following cookery methods are based on a combination of experimentation at both university and institutional levels. The value of the resulting combination is that all procedures have been first refined, then reduced to practical methods applicable to virtually all levels and types of volume feeding and well within the grasp of institutional personnel.

Our assumption in discussing meat cookery methods is that three factors should be of prime interest to the institutional cook: (1) which method will provide the largest number of portions with the greatest ease of preparation; (2) which method will assure the best possible economy; and (3) which method will produce the most acceptable quality. Related to these factors, and of critical importance, is the need to select that method which will hold meat shrinkage to a minimum while improving the product itself in terms of palatability—flavor, tenderness, and juiciness. Any properly cooked meat will rank high in palatability, and especially so if when combining with other food elements they are correctly blended into the procedure during the cooking process.

Research and practice have established that tender meats are best cooked by dry heat. Dry heat can mean cooking by heated air in an oven, by radiant heat such as broiling, or by dry frying. Less tender meats lend themselves to moist heat methods of cooking, with the meat being surrounded by hot liquid or steam vapor. With this simple rule in mind, we can go into detailed explanations of varied methods.

Roasting Beef

It is generally agreed that, with the exception of broiling, high temperatures have little, if any, place in meat cookery. Extreme, sustained heat during the roasting process will produce severe losses resulting in an end product ranked low on the palatability scale. Thus, the only standard, infallible method of roasting involves low-temperature cooking.

Meat shrinks as it cooks, no matter the method used. The amount of loss depends on the composition of the meat and the cooking method. Losses stem from two primary processes—evaporation or loss of water, and loss of fat, oils, and other extractives. Loss runs from a high of 30 percent to a low of 10 percent. Beyond the immediate problem of reduction in bulk volume caused by cooking loss, one must also consider that a roast with a high loss factor will be less palatable since it will have little moisture content. The waste will be compounded because the resulting meat will be difficult to carve; the connective tissue will be brittle, causing slices to shatter and fall apart. Dietetically it will be inferior because the vitamin-rich extractives will end up in the cooking pan or will be dissipated by vapors caused by the high heat.

The Low-Temperature Method
of Roasting

The degree to which a roast should be cooked (doneness) will also have to be considered in producing a product of ultimate quality and palatability. This factor will influence shrinkage just as will high-temperature roasting. As the degree of doneness is increased, shrinkage is increased. Meats such as pork, which are best when well-done, will continue to shrink markedly if cooked any beyond the time needed to bring them to the done stage. No meat should ever be cooked beyond this stage. The simple ratio of cooking time to roast size is not an accurate guide in determining doneness. The more accurate method is to measure the internal temperature of the meat with a thermometer.

Assuming that a relatively tender cut of meat is to be roasted, the following steps are recommended:

1. Place the roast, fat side up, on a rack in an open pan, which will allow the meat to baste itself as it cooks.
2. Do not add water and do not cover.
3. Roast at a constant, low oven temperature of 250 to 325 degrees.

4. Turn large roasts several times while cooking.
5. Remove from the heat immediately when the degree of doneness is reached.

Variations in Roasting Techniques

Some operations cooking heavy roasts which either have been rolled and tied or whole beef rib roasts use what is known as the salt shell roasting method, where meats are cooked in a bed and cover of coarse rock salt. This method has certain advantages but also the negative factor of a sometimes diminished flavor. The theory is that the salt absorbs excess oven heat and distributes it evenly during the cooking period. Steam is retained within the shell of the salt cover, producing a tenderizing effect. Among the advantages of this method is that it may allow for use of a lower grade of beef (e.g., USDA Standard against USDA Choice). The meat will retain its juices, keeping the product moist. Furthermore, the questionable tenderness of the lower grade of meat will often be raised to equal that of a higher grade. Being moist, the meat can also be held in the warming table for extended periods without becoming dry.

On the minus side, one must consider the cost of the salt cover and the possible flavor loss. This relative lack of flavor will result from the absence of a crusty exterior, which gives the meat the suggestion of having been cooked by moist heat rather than by roasting. Additionally, the correct degree of doneness will be somewhat more difficult to arrive at, making the method dependent to a certain degree on a time against weight formula.

Roasting Frozen or Deeply Chilled Meats

Practical usage has established that roasting meats from a frozen or deeply chilled state is a convenient and economical method of meat cookery for institutional use. Valuable refrigeration space is conserved by not having to allocate such space to thawing. This method also eliminates the need for advance planning, since frozen meat can go directly from freezer to oven. Just as conveniently, deeply chilled meats can go from refrigeration to oven without need for letting it reach room temperature. Cooking yields from meat cooked either from the frozen or deeply chilled state will be the same as from room-temperature meat, providing that the low-temperature method is followed during

Table 21.

Time Table for Roasting Frozen or Deeply Chilled Meats*

Item	Weight Range (pounds)	Oven Temp. (degrees)	Internal Temp. When Cooked (degrees)†	Minutes to Cook per Pound		Percentage Yield of Cooked Meat
				Frozen	Chilled	
Inside top round	10-15	300	150	30-35	20-22	76
Top sirloin	9-10	300	150	40-45	25-27	85
Rolled, boneless rib	10-12	300	150	30-32	20-25	80
Rolled chuck	12-15	300	150	30-35	20-25	80
Shoulder clod	10-12	300	150	32-35	20-25	83
Rolled leg of lamb (boneless)	4-5	325	180	45	30	60
Rolled lamb shoulder (boneless)	4-5	325	180	50	40	65
Rolled veal chuck (boneless)	10-15	325	170	35	30	78
Rolled pork shoulder	4-6	350	185	50	45	75
Pork loin (bone in)	12-15	325	185	35	30	55

*A meat thermometer will not penetrate frozen meat nor function precisely in the preliminary cooking period in deeply chilled meats. Insert the thermometer near the end of cooking period to test for state of doneness.

†The temperature range for doneness is approximately 150 degrees for medium-well to 180 degrees for well-done.

Table 22.

Meats Suitable for Open-Fire, Pan, or Griddle Broiling

Beef (Steaks)	Lamb	Pork	Veal	Variety Meats
Rib	Shoulder chops	Sliced ham	T-bones (if well-fatted)	Veal, lamb, or beef liver
				Lamb kidneys
T-bone	Rib chops			Brains
Porterhouse	Loin chops			Sweetbreads
Sirloin (Strip loin)	Leg steaks			
Tenderloin	Lamb patties			
Top Sirloin				
Top Round				
Chuck				

the cooking process. The meat will have the same palatability, crustiness, and core juiciness as that of meat roasted fresh or allowed to thaw from a frozen state before cooking.

Much meat cookery experimentation has been performed by the University of Illinois and the University of Texas in conjunction with the National Live Stock and Meat Board of Chicago using USDA Grade meats. Various tests and studies comparing roasted fresh and frozen meats for yield, palatability, and visual appearance produced favorable comparisons. To make these findings useful for institutions where more economical grades of meat are used Table 21 was compiled. It is designed for use with meats below Choice Grade. This chart gives a cooking timetable and oven temperature guide for USDA Standard and USDA Commercial meat grades.

Table 23.
Timetable for Open-Fire Broiling
(Charcoal, Gas-Heated Filaments, or
Electrical Heating Elements)

Cut of Meat	Thickness	Rare* (minutes)	Medium* (minutes)	Well-done* (minutes)
Rib, T-bone, porterhouse, sirloin strip, tenderloin, top sirloin, top round, or chuck steaks	1 inch	15	20	25
	1½ inches	20	30	35+
	2 inches	35	45	Not recommended
Ground beef patties or steaks	1 inch	15	20	25+
Ground lamb patties	1 inch		20	25+
Smoked ham slice	½ inch			12
	1 inch			18
Bacon, thick cut				4+
Chateaubriand (tenderloin)		30	50+	Not recommended

*Meat should be turned after one-half the cooking time indicated.

Meats below the grade of USDA Choice have marked advantages regarding shrinkage, although they will not produce a finished product of equal tenderness. Cutting losses from lower grade meats are approximately 10 percent less than from Choice, and this improves as the meat cools. (Normal tempering time for hot roasts is 20 to 30 minutes.) The greatest comparative advantage is reached after the meat has been refrigerated and is sliced cold. Lower grade meats will then produce approximately 15 percent more sliced product than will the higher grades. This is because USDA Standard and Commercial Grades have more actual muscle meat and less fat per pound than meats of the upper grades. Much shrinkage of Choice or Prime Grade meat is brought about by fat loss and evaporation of the more abundant internal juices.

Broiling Meats

Meat selected for broiling should be restricted to high grade cuts which have a natural tenderness. Beef should be in the form of well fatted cuts from USDA Good Grade or better. Certain well-aged lower grades which are tenderized by marination or with commercial tenderizers can also be broiled with a relative degree of success. Tenderized meat, however, should be seared quickly so that the meat retains its juiciness. Veal cuts are not recommended for broiling because of their low fat content. An exception is the veal T-bone which may be pan- or griddle-broiled if they are of high quality and contain sufficient fat cover.

Recommended cuts for broiling include all cuts of tender beef steak, ground meat patties of any kind, lamb chops, mutton chops, and thick ham steaks. Pork does not lend itself to broiling; braising or frying are better methods.

Broiling employs intense heat. This can be produced by charcoal, gas fired cookers with ceramic rocks, or an electric element. Gas or electric broilers with an overhead flame are also effective. Regardless of which broiling device is used the end result will be identical, for no type of cooker has the ability to inject flavor. The broiling process is converse to that used in roasting. In broiling, meat is cooked as rapidly as possible, for it is the crustiness of the meat that produces the flavor sensation.

Open-Fire Broiling

Intense carmelization of broiled beef is achieved by bringing the cooking device to its highest heat point. If the meat is seasoned before cooking the seasoning will become part of the crustiness, adding richly to its flavor. Salt will slow the carmelization process slightly and therefore should be added after the meat has been turned and the first side is well seared. Broiled meat should be turned only once. Further turning or disturbing the meat as it cooks interrupts the process and slows down the carmelization. The meat should be placed as near the heating material or element as possible. The first side should be quickly browned and seared to create a seal. This prevents juices from oozing into the fire below or going up in smoke if the heating element is above. When the meat is turned the juices will rise to the center of the meat. The crustiness of the first side will prevent it from escaping. Additional turning will drive the juices to the bottom where they may escape, leaving the meat dry and less flavorful.

Although the broiling process is common to open-fire cookery, it need not be that restrictive. In essence the act of broiling involves searing the meat to form a flavorful crust through direct exposure to intense heat. Two alternative methods exist. One is pan broiling, the other is griddle broiling.

Pan and Griddle Broiling

Pan broiling can be every bit as effective as open-fire broiling and is used by some of the finest restaurants. A heavy commercial type cast iron skillet is ideal for this process. Those treated with nonstick coatings will not produce a worthwhile product; intense heat will destroy the coating and transfer bits of it to the meat. Heat the skillet intensely before starting to cook. Add no fat—just cook the meat dry as though it were on an open fire. As in open-fire broiling, the meat should be seasoned, then cooked quickly to a fine crust with only one turning. There will be no discernible difference in flavor between this and the open-fire process. The meat's appearance may differ slightly, however, since open fired broilers will enhance the crusty coating and color of the finished product. As the pan is reused, any drippings should be drained away. A collection of fats in the pan will tend to produce a less tender steak with an additional loss of color and crispness. Grill or griddle broiling is much the same as pan broiling, employing a heavy grill, high heat, and no cooking fats.

Braising Meats

Braising is a method of cooking with moist heat. The meat is first browned in a small amount of fat and then cooked with a small amount of liquid. The method also includes potroasting and fricasseeing. This method is used extensively in low-budget cookery since it is

Table 24.
Meats Suitable for Braising

Beef	*Lamb*	*Pork*	*Veal*	*Variety Meats*
Chuck	Breast	Chops	Breast	Heart
Brisket	Neck	Shoulder	Shoulder	Beef or pork
Flank	Shanks	Hocks	Neck	liver
Round		Spareribs	Shank	Kidneys
Shank				Tripe
Short ribs				
Oxtails				

Table 25.
Timetable for Braising Meats

Cut	*Size*	*Approximate Cooking Time (hours)*
Beef chuck, untied	3-5 pounds	3-4
Beef chuck, rolled	5-12 pounds	4-5
Beef Swiss steaks	1 inch thick	2½-3
Beef flank steak	½ inch thick	1-1½
Stuffed steak	¾ inch thick	1½
Beef shortribs	cut in sections	2-2½
Beef birds	½ x 2 x 4 or 5 in.	1½-2
Stuffed lamb breast	2-4 pounds	1½-2
Lamb breast	1 section	1½-2
Lamb neck	whole	1½-2
Lamb riblets	cut in sections	2½-3
Pork chops	¾ to 1 inch	¾
Spareribs	cut in sections	1½
Veal Pot-roast	3-5 pounds	3 hours
Veal breast	1 section	2½
Veal birds	rolled and skewered	1
Fricassee, beef	cut in 1-inch cubes	2-3
Fricassee, veal	cut in 1-inch cubes	2
Fricassee, pork	cut in 1-inch cubes	1½

applicable to less tender, more economical cuts of meat. Meats cooked by the braising method will retain their natural juices and will not dry out. Braising, which is a lengthy process, also breaks down connective tissues and tenderizes even the toughest meats.

The steps in braising are as follows:

1. Dredge the meat with flour containing the necessary seasonings. Then brown, regardless of the size of cut. A heavy coating of flour produces a sauce for use as a gravy. If a large amount of sauce is required, thickening must be added during or after cooking.
2. Add a small amount of liquid. With meat cubed to be used for stew, the liquid should only be sufficient to partly submerge the meat.
3. Cover with tight fitting lid.
4. Bring the liquid to a simmer, then reduce the heat to the lowest point which will sustain a slow, bubbling simmer.
5. Cook until the meat is tender. A large pot roast or section of meat should have an internal heat of between 185 and 195 degrees.

Simmering and Stewing Meats

Simmering also employs moist heat. Frequently the process is referred to as boiling, although there is a difference between the two methods. In simmering, the meat is submerged in the cooking liquid, but it is cooked below the boiling point. Cooking at heat higher than simmering destroys certain taste qualities which affect palatability. It also causes undue shrinkage and fragmentation, for the outside parts of the meat cook more rapidly than the inner, often tougher, parts. Simmering requires full flavored, robust cuts, because some of the flavor escapes into the surrounding liquids during the cooking process. Such liquids can, of course, be used as a base for highly flavored and highly nutritious soups or as a base for sauces or gravies, as well as for cooking vegetables.

The difference between simmering and stewing relates to the size of the cut and the purpose for which it is intended. Simmering is usually employed with large cuts or whole pieces of meats where the resulting liquid will be strictly a by-product. Stewing involves smaller pieces where the liquid will form an integral part of the recipe and where other ingredients will be added during the cooking.

The steps for simmering are the following:

1. Immerse the meat in water or seasoned stock along with any desired seasonings such as herbs, spices, salt, and pepper.
2. Bring to a boil and reduce heat to a simmer.
3. Cover and cook until tender.

The steps in stewing are as follows:

1. Cut meat to desired size.
2. For brown stew, dredge meat in flour and brown over a high heat to form a good color.
3. Cover generously with liquid and bring to a boil, reducing heat to a simmer.
4. Add any basic seasonings desired.
5. Cook until slightly tender.
6. Add any combination of vegetables, first adding those requiring long cooking, then proceeding to add others which cook quickly, so that when the last vegetables are done the stew will be finished.
7. If a thickening is desired add roux and continue to simmer until the proper thickness is attained and the roux is thoroughly cooked.
8. Adjust seasonings.

Chicken Stock

(yield: approximately 3 gallons)

Chicken, stewing hen, or cock, 5 or 6 lbs.	1
Cold water	5 gal.
Celery pieces and tops	3 cups
Carrots, unpeeled and quartered	6
Onions, large, unpeeled and quartered	2
Peppercorns	1 tbsp.
Bay leaves, small	2
Parsley, bunch	½

Method: Put all ingredients into a stock pot and bring to a boil. Reduce to a simmer for 3 to 4 hours or until the liquid is reduced to about 3 gallons. Reserve the cooked chicken for other purposes. Skim and strain the liquid. Refrigerate if not needed immediately.

Added chicken fat, cracked chicken legs, or chicken bones will enrich the stock considerably.

Beef Stock

(yield: approximately 5 gallons)

Beef bones, trimmings, or pieces	10 lbs.
Cold water	10 gal.
Bay leaves, small	2
Peppercorns	2 tbsp.
Celery tops and pieces	1 qt.
Onions, quartered	6
Carrots, unpeeled and quartered	6
Parsley, bunch	1

Method: Bring the stock to a boil. Reduce to a simmer for 8 to 12 hours or until liquid is reduced by half. Skim frequently during the cooking period and strain before using.

For continuous use it will not be necessary to change the stock pot if it is kept cooking at a simmer. Additional liquid, trimmings and vegetable pieces can be added at any time, with the water being replaced as it is drained off. Such a pot will be effective from 2 to 3 days without changing. If the stock should cool it will be necessary to place it under refrigeration or begin a new pot since the liquid will sour in a short period of time at room temperature. The prepared stock will keep well for 4 to 5 days under refrigeration.

Table 26.
Meat Cuts for Simmering or Stewing

Beef	*Lamb*	*Pork*	*Veal*	*Variety*
Chuck	Neck	Spareribs	Neck	Kidney
Leg shanks	Breast	Feet	Shank	Heart
Brisket (fresh)	Flank	Hocks	Breast	Tongue
(corned)	Shanks	Ham	Flank	Tripe
Plate		Picnics		
Flank		Shoulder butt		
Short ribs				
Bottom round (corned)				

Table 27.
Timetable for Simmering or Stewing

Cut	Size	Approximate Cooking Time (hours)
Fresh beef	5-9 pounds	4
Fresh beef	1 inch cubes	2-1/2-3
Corned beef		
Brisket	4-5 pounds	4
Round	5-8 pounds	6
Smoked hams	8-16 pounds	1/3 per pound
Stew, lamb, veal,		
or pork	1 inch cubes	2
Veal, fresh	various	2
Lamb, fresh	various	2

Table 28.
Internal Temperatures for Different Degrees
of Doneness*

Type of Meat	State of Doneness	Internal Temperature (degrees)
Beef roast	rare	140
Beef roast	medium	160
Beef roast	well-done	170
Lamb roast	well-done	180
Pork roast	well-done	185
Whole cured ham	well-done	160
Veal roast	well-done	170

*Most good meat thermometers show meat temperatures and doneness on their faces.

Frying or Sauteing Meats

Frying can best be defined as the process of cooking in a fat or cooking oil. The basic process is an extension of the dry heat method of cooking and there are several variations. It is appropriate only with tender meats which can be cooked quickly, to produce a flavorful crust, or stir-fried (sauteing), a method used when meats and other ingredients are cooked together and a crusting is not necessary. Meats ideal for pan-frying are any steak material cut thin and made tender by pounding, scoring, or cubing: laminated steaks (very thin slices of meat compressed to form a patty/cubed veal, pork or lamb cutlets, sliced liver, sweetbreads, brains, ham, bacon, and sausage.

Deep-fat frying cooks meats in a volume of surrounding cooking fat at temperatures of between 350 and 375 degrees. Since this is a rapid cooking process only the tenderest cuts should be used, and they should be well-breaded and coated. Meats appropriate for deep-fat frying include laminated steaks, veal, pork or lamb cutlets, cubed beef steaks, sweetbreads, liver, and brains. Since only thinner cuts can be cooked in this manner, the most reliable way to determine that they are done is when the outside breading or coating is well-browned.

Steam Cooking Methods for Meats

Nonpressure or steam type cookers offer certain advantages over the pressurized type. Although they require approximately 10 to 20 percent more time for cooking meat, they are capable of handling larger cuts. Furthermore, they have a tenderizing effect on tougher cuts and produce a juicier finished product. Pot roasts or other rolled and tied sections should be cooked 12 to 15 minutes per pound to produce a medium-well to well-done product. Corned beef requires 20 to 25 minutes per pound. The time for stews or meats surrounded by liquid depends on its relative tenderness. USDA Standard or Commercial Grade of meats used in economy dishes should be cooked 15 minutes per gross pound. If meat is to be taken directly from the steamer to a warming table for a holding period of an hour or more, it should be cooked 3 minutes less per pound. Meat continues to cook if the holding table is maintained at a temperature of 150 degrees or more, causing some deterioration in texture.

Pressure Cooking

Pressure cooking uses superheated live steam at a temperature above the boiling point. This high heat, coupled with the pressure generated in the cooker, drives the heat into the meat, producing very rapid cooking action. Not recommended for cuts larger than 4 to 5 lbs.

In pressure cooking the heat generated will be 228 degrees at 5 pounds of pressure, 240 degrees at 10 pounds and 250 degrees at 15 pounds. The desired pressure is reached more rapidly if the liquid added to the cooker is warm or hot before cooking begins. Most cookers are equipped with safety valves to release pressure in excess of 15 pounds. Safety devices and gauges should be checked regularly when such cookers are in use to ensure that they are working properly.

Microwave Cooking

This new type of cooking is rapidly evolving into forms which are applicable to institutional use, although it is still unsuitable for volume food production. Currently its most widespread commercial application is in the fast food business, where frozen or refrigerated foods can be almost instantly reconstituted for rapid service. Microwaves produce no external heat. Instead they penetrate only the item being cooked. Although penetration in most cookers is limited to from 3 to 3½ inches, new sophisticated cookers are now being introduced which continue the cooking process by conduction, producing a uniform product by using two distinct processes of cooking simultaneously.

Both the installation and methodology of microwave cookery require the advice of specialists in this emerging field. Microwave equipment dealers are best able to provide guidance about cost, feasibility, and applications.

Cooking Variety and Less Tender
Cuts of Meat

Meats from both these categories can be used to advantage in producing upgraded menu items. Variety meats particularly have good public acceptance because of their high flavors and can be used to prepare highly palatable dishes. The tendonous cuts of muscle meat also have a robust flavor and are versatile far beyond their basic use in producing rich stocks and broths. Both types of meat are relatively low in cost and can therefore be used to advantage for low-cost menu items.

The classes of variety meats are: liver, tongue, sweetbreads, heart, kidney, brains, tripe, and oxtail. They are all rich in protein, iron, and vitamins A, B, and C.

Liver

Beef and calf liver are generally more acceptable menu items than pork and lamb liver, although the latter two are fully as nutritious and potent in iron and vitamins. Pork liver has a strong flavor while lamb is the blandest of all livers. Beef livers weighing more than 12 pounds probably come from bulls or old cows and will tend to be tough. Calf (sometimes listed as veal) livers range from 2 to 8 pounds, according to the age of the animal. Those under 2 pounds are likely to be mushy and/or flavorless. All liver can be precooked for volume recipes and will not toughen when held in the warming table.

Sweetbreads

Generally, only calf's or lamb's sweetbreads are used in cookery although beef sweetbreads may be used when mixed with other meats. These meats must be either very fresh or frozen since they diminish in acceptability very rapidly. (Freezing has no effect on their palatability.) They may be fried, sauteed, or braised after first being simmered to ease removal of the outer membrane.

Hearts

Beef, veal, lamb, and pork hearts are all edible and interchangeable in most recipes. They are the least expensive of the variety meats but require more attention during preparation than other variety cuts. Because they are all relatively tough they must be prepared by long, slow methods of moist cooking.

Kidneys

Beef, veal, pork, and lamb kidneys are high in nutrition and are suitable for many methods of preparation. Beef kidneys are the least tender and have the strongest flavor. All, however, require long periods of cooking and are most often braised or stewed. Veal or lamb kidneys from young animals may be broiled and are often incorporated in, or served with, veal chops or lamb chops.

Tongue

Tongue dishes almost always incorporate beef or veal tongues, primarily because they are large enough to slice. They are available fresh, smoked, and sweet-pickled. All require long periods of cooking by moist heat.

Tripe

Although tripe comes precooked, it requires prolonged periods of moist cooking to make it tender and edible. Honeycomb tripe is used in most recipes. Tripe is the least desirable of the variety meats, save as an ingredient in pepperpot soup. It is also used in such ethnic dishes as Mexican menudo or Tripe a la mode de Caen.

Tendonous or Less-tender
Cuts of Meat

The use of brisket, foreshank, and shoulder clod of beef or veal can keep food costs low while producing acceptable and nutritious entrees. The foreshank has a large amount of connective tissue which makes it tough, requiring prolonged moist heat for tenderization. Often the shanks are cross-sawed into portions and simmered in water to produce a rich, robust stock. They can then be boned, with the meat being used in stews, meat pies, or similar dishes. The clod, while neither as tough or tissue-filled, will also require considerable moist heat cooking, although a veal clod may be used for a marginal roast if cooked by the prolonged low-heat method. The brisket is more useful than either of the above cuts and is most frequently employed in making corned beef. It is highly flavorful and tender when cooked by moist heat.

21.

Economies Through the Use of Meat Extenders

In certain situations meats may be extended with commercially prepared extenders or with bread crumbs, oatmeal, or potatoes. Commercially prepared extenders usually have a soy bean or wheat base plus additional flavoring. They are both nutritious and wholesome; at least one is used as a low cost meat substitute in vegetarian diets. These products should be used in accordance with manufacturers' directions for best results.

Extenders created in the kitchen should be employed only in moderation. Wholesome, nutritive substances should be used, those that will not in any manner diminish the food value of the product. The extender should never obviously announce its presence; indeed, every effort should be made to produce a superior flavored product rather than merely a cheaper one. In certain recipes the addition to beef products of other meats such as chicken or pork will enhance the taste and result in an end product that is not only more economical but actually improved in nutritive values. Meat loaves, chili, and other similar dishes, often contain extenders to increase the bulk of the recipe. Here they not only serve an economical purpose but also add to taste, flavor, and consistency. This is particularly true of the majority of chili dishes.

Another situation where extenders serve an important purpose beyond their economy is in hamburger products where rapid service is involved. Extended hamburger patties or steaks prepared ahead of the service period will keep their shape and flavor for several hours and will not have a precooked appearance. Sandwich patties can be pre-cooked in slack periods for instant service during peak rushes. The same style of service also has obvious advantages for institutions, where precooked hamburger steaks can be readied in advance of feeding peaks. This is accomplished by cooking the steaks to a medium degree of doneness to allow for continued cooking while being held. They are then placed in warming table trays containing beef stock which maintains the moisture content while they are kept ready for serving. Leftover meat loaves, patties, and steaks made with ground meats and containing extenders can be stored under refrigeration by keeping them in liquid or wrapping them in moist towels. They will retain their texture, flavor, and appearance to a greater degree than will pure meat products and can be reheated with no shrinkage loss.

It should be noted that state and local regulations sometimes require commercial restaurants to mention clearly on the menu that extenders have been used. This is not generally the case with meat loaves, chilis, or similar dishes where extenders are a basic and integral part of the recipe. Nor will the inclusion of extenders have to be noted in hamburger products labeled "King Burger," "Dan Burger," etc.

The following recipes offer examples of how to extend ground meat products.

Bread Extended Hamburger Mix

(yield: 26 pounds)

Ground beef	18 lbs.
Ground pork	6 lbs.
Salt	½ cup
Ground black pepper	4 tsp.
Onions, grated or chopped fine	2 cups
Milk	2 cups
Fine, dry bread crumbs	2 qts.
Monosodium glutamate	2 tbsp.

Method: Mix all ingredients, blending until smooth and evenly mixed. Refrigerate well before forming into patties or steaks. Cook at a low temperature to retain moisture and flavor. No additional seasoning will be needed.

Both the bread crumbs and the pork, which can be economical trimmings from the shoulder or other cuts of the low cost variety, act as extenders. The milk adds moisture to make the mixture flavorful and improve its texture.

Potato Beefburger Mix

(yield: 12 pounds)

Ground beef	6 lbs.
Well-scrubbed, unpeeled potatoes, coarsely grated or ground	3 qts.
Onion, grated or chopped fine	1 cup
Salt	3 tbsp.
Ground black pepper	1 tsp.
Monosodium glutamate	2 tbsp.

Method: Combine all ingredients and mix well to form a smooth, even blend. Refrigerate well before shaping. Cook at low temperatures to retain moisture.

Hamburger patties or steaks can be either fully or partially cooked prior to serving time and reheated quickly for fast service or volume feeding.

Chili con Carne, Extended

(yield: 3 gallons)

Red, kidney, or chili beans, canned	1½ No. 10 can (or 3 No. 5 cans)
Coarsely ground beef	4 lbs.
Beef fat	1 cup
Onions, chopped fine	2 cups
Tomatoes, canned	1½ No. 10 can (or 3 No. 5 cans)
Salt	4 tbsp.
Red chili powder	8 tbsp.
Ground cumins	4 tsp.
Monosodium glutamate	2 tbsp.
Rolled oats (not quick cooking)	4 cups
Flour	2 cups
Water	2 cups

Method: Drain beans and reserve liquid. Sauté beef in melted fat until brown. Add onions and cook until soft. Add tomatoes, salt, chili powder, cumins, MSG, and rolled oats. Simmer over a low heat for 1 hour. Mix flour, heat liquid and water and add. Stir well. Continue cooking for 10 minutes or until the mixture thickens. Stir in beans. Remove from heat.

This mixture may be refrigerated and heated as required by placing over hot water in a double boiler or brought to temperature suitable for serving by placing in the warming table 2 hours before serving time.

22.

Vegetarian Feeding, Meatless Preparations, and Meat Substitutes

Vegetarian feeding is a special branch of food preparation which avoids in its cookery any meat products or injected meat flavors. For the most part it is restricted to those situations where the consumer will reject a dish if it offers any suggestion of meat products or flavoring. Meatless preparations and meat substitutes, on the other hand, are those foods which can carry meat injected flavor as well as a certain amount of meat for flavoring a preparation which would otherwise be flat or unattractive. The sample recipes in this chapter are not intended for vegetarian cookery. They are instead recipes which can be used in all kinds of meat controlled programs where the intent is to create an acceptable variety menu item. Beyond being well suited to low-budget cookery, these foods have a high rate of acceptability, for they are both palatable and nutritious.

Fried Cornmeal Mush

	25 portions	*100 portions*
Hot water	1 gal.	4 gals.
Salt	1½ tbsp.	6 tbsp.
Yellow cornmeal	5 cups	20 cups
Cold water	1 qt.	1 gal.

Method: Add salt to hot water and bring to a boil. Combine corn-meal with cold water and gradually add to the boiling, salted water while stirring constantly to keep from lumping. Lower heat and cook at a simmer for 15 minutes, stirring frequently. Remove from heat and pour into 1 pound loaf pans and chill for 8 to 12 hours.

Service: Slice into ½ inch pieces and fry on a lightly greased grill until golden brown on both sides.

Note: Fried mush, which can be prepared in volume by oven fry-ing, makes an ideal base for such items as creamed boiled eggs, creamed chicken, or creamed tuna. It can also be used in place of steamed rice or noodles for a change in pace for single plate entrees where the meat is placed on top, such as for braises of all kinds, or for veal or pork cutlets. For dietary enrichment mix ½ cup dry milk solids to each 25 portions of mush just before combining with the cold water.

Spaghetti with Cheese and Eggs

	25 portions	50 portions
Spaghetti, uncooked	2½ lbs.	5 lbs.
Water for cooking	as required	as required
Butter or oleomargarine	1 lb.	2 lbs.
Flour	1 lb.	2 lbs.
Salt	1 tbsp.	2 tbsp.
White pepper	1 tsp.	2 tsp.
Prepared mustard	½ cup	1 cup
Milk	1 gal.	2 gals.
Cheddar cheese, grated	2 lbs.	4 lbs.
Green pepper, chopped fine	1 pt.	1 qt.
Pimiento, chopped small	½ pt.	1 pt.
Hard boiled eggs, diced	12	24
Monosodium glutamate	1 tbsp.	2 tbsp.
Pitted ripe olives, sliced	½ pt.	1 pt.

Method: Break spaghetti into 2-inch lengths and cook according to package directions. Drain well. Melt butter and stir in flour, salt, pep-per, and mustard, mixing well. Add milk gradually, stirring constantly to keep the mixture smooth, cooking until it thickens. Stir in cheese, green peppers, pimiento, diced eggs, and MSG, mixing well. Add cooked spaghetti and pour into well greased baking pans. Sprinkle with ripe olives and paprika if desired. Bake in 350° oven for 45 minutes.

Service: Eight ounces for a single plate entree.

Note: This recipe may be enriched by adding 1 cup dry milk solids along with the flour.

Mexican Style Stuffed Green Peppers

	25 portions	*50 portions*
Large green peppers	25	50
Cooked rice	2 qts.	1 gal.
Onions, chopped fine	2 cups	4 cups
Clarified butter or oleomargarine	4 tbsp.	8 tbsp.
Whole kernel corn, drained	1 No. 2½ can	1 No. 5 can
Canned tomatoes, chopped	2 lbs.	4 lbs.
Chili powder	1 tbsp.	2 tbsp.
Monosodium glutamate	1 tbsp.	2 tbsp.
Salt	1 tbsp.	2 tbsp.
White pepper	½ tsp.	1 tsp.
Seasoned bread crumbs	1 cup	2 cups
Meat stock or warm water	1 qt.	2 qts.

Method: Cut tops from peppers and remove seeds. Add chopped pepper tops to the onions and sauté in butter until the onions are soft. Add whole kernel corn, tomatoes, chili powder, MSG, salt, and pepper and combine with cooked rice, mixing well. Pack stuffing into peppers and sprinkle with seasoned bread crumbs. Place peppers in baking pan, pouring the stock or warm water around the edges so as not to disturb topping. Bake in 350 degree oven for 1 hour or until peppers are tender.

Service: One pepper per portion.

Baked Noodles and Tomatoes, Mexican Style

	25 portions	*50 portions*
Cooked wide noodles	6 lbs. (2 lbs. uncooked)	12 lbs. (4 lbs. uncooked)
Butter or oleomargarine	½ cup	1 cup
Onions, chopped fine	1 cup	2 cups
Green peppers, chopped coarse	2 cups	4 cups
Tomatoes, cubed	5 lbs.	10 lbs.
Salt	1 tbsp.	2 tbsp.
Chili powder	1 tbsp.	2 tbsp.
Cheddar cheese, grated	2 lbs.	4 lbs.
Bread crumbs	2 cups	4 cups
Paprika	as required	as required

Method: Melt butter and sauté onions, green pepper, and tomatoes, cooking until vegetables are soft. Add salt and chili powder and mix well. Combine cooked noodles and tomato mixture and place in individual 8 ounce casseroles or in a baking pan. Sprinkle the mixture first with grated cheese, then bread crumbs. Sprinkle lightly with paprika. Bake in 375 degree oven for 30 minutes or until topping is lightly browned and the mixture well heated.

Note: This recipe can be prepared in advance and held. Bake just before transferring to the warming table.

Cheese Cutlets

	25 portions	50 portions
Butter or oleomargarine	8 oz.	1 lb.
Flour	1 cup	2 cups
Hot milk	2 qts.	1 gal.
Salt	2 tsp.	4 tsp.
White pepper	1 tsp.	2 tsp.
Cayenne	pinch	pinch
Paprika	1 tbsp.	2 tbsp.
Dry mustard	1 tbsp.	2 tbsp.
Fine, dry bread crumbs	1 qt.	2 qts.
Cheddar cheese, grated	3 lbs.	6 lbs.
Eggs, slightly beaten	4	8
Flour, seasoned with salt	as required	as required

Method: Melt butter and add flour, simmering until smooth and well mixed. Gradually add hot milk, continuing to simmer until the mixture is thick and smooth. Add salt, pepper, cayenne, paprika and dry mustard. Mix well. Combine grated cheese and crumbs and add, simmering long enough to melt the cheese. Remove from heat and whip in the eggs. Allow to cool and form into 3-ounce cutlets. To serve, roll cutlets in seasoned flour and pan fry or grill.

For volume production the cutlets may also be oven fried by placing them on a well greased cooking sheet and cooking at 375 degrees until well browned.

Service: Two cutlets on an underlining of white sauce or tomato sauce.

Spanish-Style Macaroni

	25 portions	*100 portions*
Green peppers, chopped small	1 pt.	2 qts.
Shortening	½ cup	2 cups
Flour	½ cup	2 cups
Hot milk	6½ pts.	2½ gals.
Salt	1 tsp.	4 tsp.
Ground black pepper	1 tsp.	4 tsp.
Dry mustard	1 tbsp.	4 tbsp.
Cheddar cheese, grated	1¼ lb.	5 lbs.
Cut elbow macaroni, uncooked	1¼ lb.	5 lbs.
Salted boiling water	as required	as required
Stuffed olives, sliced	½ pt.	1 qt.
Corn flakes, rolled and crushed	3 ozs.	12 ozs.
Melted butter or oleomargarine	1 tbsp.	4 tbsp.

Method: Cook green pepper in melted shortening until soft. Stir in flour and mix well. Add to hot milk and cook at a simmer until the mixture is thickened and smooth. Add salt, pepper, dry mustard, and cheddar cheese, continuing to simmer until the cheese is melted. Cook macaroni in boiling salted water until tender. Drain and rinse well. Lay alternate layers of cooked macaroni, sauce, and sliced olives in a baking pan to form a mixture 2 inches thick. Mix corn flakes and butter and sprinkle over the top. Bake in 250 degree oven for 45 minutes.

Service: eight ounces for a single plate entree.

Note: Enrichment may be achieved by adding 1 cup dry milk solids to each 25 portions as the milk is being cooked and thickened.

23.

Sandwiches

The sandwiches in this section are designed to be used as entrees. They illustrate kinds that can be volume produced and prepared in advance. They have a high nutritional value and comply fully with the Type A feeding program specifications. Each has sufficient food value to sustain a person from one meal to another if served with a beverage and augmented with a simple dessert or a piece of fruit.

For fast service sandwiches of this kind can be either individually wrapped and stored under refrigeration for 24 hours or stacked two high on trays and covered with a light cloth and held in refrigeration for several hours.

For estimating the necessary bread requirement a 24-ounce loaf of institutional sandwich bread will yield an average of 30 slices.

Meat Spread Sandwiches

	25 portions	*50 portions*
Cooked ground meat	1 qt.	2 qts.
Sweet pickles, chopped fine	1½ cups	3 cups
Onion, chopped fine	½ cup	1 cup
Prepared mustard	½ cup	1 cup
Celery, chopped fine	1½ cups	3 cups
Mayonnaise	1½ cups	3 cups

Method: Combine all ingredients well to form a smooth spread. Use 2½ ounces for each portion. Variety can be achieved by alternating the kind of bread used if the sandwiches are used regularly.

The meat content of these sandwiches can be ground cooked ham, corned beef, roast beef, chicken, or turkey. The bread will not require any additional spread, making production more rapid. If the sandwiches are to be used immediately they can be served with a leaf of lettuce. Do not use lettuce if they are made ahead of time for storage since it will become wilted and bitter to the taste.

Fresh Vegetable Filling

	25 portions	50 portions
Cabbage, grated	1½ lb.	3 lbs.
Carrots, grated	1 lb.	2 lbs.
Radishes, sliced thin	1 lb.	2 lbs.
Green onions, chopped fine	¼ lb.	½ lb.
Celery, chopped fine	1 lb.	2 lbs.
Green pepper, chopped fine	½ lb.	1 lb.
Cucumber, peeled and chopped	1 lb.	2 lbs.
Salt	2 tbsp.	4 tbsp.
Mayonnaise	1½ pts.	1½ qts.

Method: Combine all ingredients, mixing until the mayonnaise is well integrated. Use 4 ounces for each portion. No additional spread is needed on the bread. Alternate kinds of breads for variety.

Vegetable Club Sandwich

	25 portions	50 portions
Cabbage, shredded	2½ pts.	2½ qts.
Carrots, shredded	1¼ pts.	1¼ qts.
Cucumber, peeled and chopped	1¼ pts.	1¼ qts.
Radishes, sliced thin	1 cup	2 cups
Salt	1 tbsp.	2 tbsp.
Mayonnaise	1 pt.	1 qt.
Cheese, 1 oz. slices	25	50
Butter, olemargarine, or mayonnaise	as required	as required

Method: Combine vegetables and salt and mix with mayonnaise. For each sandwich spread bottom slice of bread with butter, oleomargarine, or mayonnaise and add slice of cheese. Top with one slice of bread. Add 4 ounces vegetable mix and top with a third slice of bread. Cut diagonally for each in serving. If sandwiches are to be served immediately, top cheese with a slice of tomato and a leaf of lettuce.

Egg Salad Spread

	25 portions	*50 portions*
Eggs, hard-boiled	24	48
Salt	2 tsp.	4 tsp.
Mayonnaise	3 cups	6 cups
Lemon juice	1 tbsp.	2 tbsp.

Method: Chill eggs, peel off shells, and chop fine. Add salt, mayonnaise, and lemon juice and work into a smooth spread. Use 3 ounces for each portion. No additional spread on bread is required.

Bacon and Cheese Spread

	25 portions	*50 portions*
Cheddar cheese, grated	4 lbs.	8 lbs.
Onion, chopped very fine	½ lb.	1 lb.
Bacon, cooked and chopped fine	½ lb.	1 lb.
Catsup	1 pt.	1 qt.
Prepared mustard	1 cup	2 cups

Method: Combine all ingredients into a smooth spread. For a cold sandwich spread 4 ounces on the bottom slice of bread and add mayonnaise to the top slice. For a hot sandwich spread the mixture on a piece of toast and arrange any number of slices on a cooking sheet and heat in a 350 degree oven for 10 minutes. Cover with a buttered top slice and heat for another 5 minutes. Remove from oven and serve at once or keep hot in the warming table during the serving period. The sandwiches will keep in the table for approximately 15 minutes without becoming soggy.

If a large number are to be served in a continuous manner the oven heating should proceed in a steady manner to stay close to the actual need by serving one lot while another is warming.

Tuna Salad Spread

	25 portions	*50 portions*
Tuna, water pack, 13 oz. cans	2	4
Lemon juice	4 tbsp.	8 tbsp.
Onion, chopped fine	½ cup	1 cup
Celery, chopped fine	1 cup	2 cups
Mayonnaise	1 pt.	1 qt.

Method: Combine all ingredients into a smooth spread. Use 2½ ounces for each portion. No additional spread will be needed on the bread. If sandwiches are to be served immediately, add a slice of tomato and a leaf of lettuce.

Water Cress and Cream Cheese Spread

	25 portions	*50 portions*
Water cress, washed and chopped fine	6 bunches	12 bunches
Cream cheese	3 lbs.	6 lbs.

Method: Allow cream cheese to sit at room temperature to soften. Mix in water cress to make an even spread. Use 2 ounces for each portion. No other spread on the bread will be required. If sandwiches are to be served immediately they may be served with lettuce and tomato slice.

24.

The Use of Seafoods in Low-Budget Cookery

Although certain seafoods have reached price cycle peaks which make them unsuitable for low-budget cookery, there remain many seafood items which can be used to produce economical, palatable, and nutritious entrees. With seafood the yield per pound is considerably higher than "red meat" foods and slightly higher than poultry. Most boneless fillets or fletches of fish will yield three generous portions per pound, four more economical portions, or five portions suitable either for dietetic use or in programs comparable to the Type A school lunch program. Portions in each instance will be less costly than other foods with similar protein value. Furthermore, seafoods lend themselves to a wide variety of cooking methods and recipes, providing excellent opportunities for expanding menu variety. All seafood cookery has one axiom: never overcook. All seafoods reach perfection when cooked exactly to the done state. Because of seafood's tenderness, overcooking quickly causes dryness and fragmentation.

Any fish or shellfish can be baked. If it is to be stuffed, the cavity should be no more than 2/3 full. Place the fish in a shallow, well-greased pan and bake at 400 degrees. Lean fish should be basted once or twice during the process. Breaded fish sticks, fillets, and steaks can be oven-fried in shallow, well-greased pans. Allow space between each piece for overall browning to take place. This method is adaptable to situations where a large number of fried servings are to be readied in a short time. Any fish fried in this manner, whether breaded or plain, will keep well in warming table trays without fragmentation for a period of 1 hour if the table temperature is approximately 150 degrees.

For broiling, thin fillets should be well greased and cooked on one side only, allowing them to remain on the broiler until cooked through. Steaks or slabs may be broiled on both sides. Turn the fish only once when the first side is well-colored and the cooking time is approximately half completed. After the fish is turned it should be basted with oil or butter to keep the juices intact and to enhance the taste.

Deep-fat frying works best with thin fillets, breaded or coated with flour or cracker meal. This also applies to shrimp. Cooking fat for both should be maintained at a temperature of 375 degrees. The item can be considered done when the coating is well browned.

Seafoods may be poached, never boiled. The liquid should first be brought to a boil, the fish placed in the pan and the water immediately dropped to a slow simmer. Use only enough liquid to cover the fish or surround it generously. Steaming in nonpressure, free venting steamers is another effective method of fish cookery. The fish should be placed dry in cooking pans. Thin fillets will cook in approximately 10 minutes, thicker steaks in 15 minutes. Whole fish require 20 minutes per pound. Both simmering and steaming produce a bland taste. For enhancement, simmered fish can be cooked in court-bouillon with seasonings added. Steamed fish should be seasoned before placing in the cooking pans. To prepare creamed seafood dishes with vegetable extenders, cook the extenders first and add the seafood during the last few minutes of cooking. As an alternative, the creamed portion of the recipe and the seafood may be cooked separately and then combined. This prevents fragmentation and overcooking. The fish should be stirred in gently and the preparation removed immediately from the fire.

25.

Vegetable Cookery

Regardless of how vegetables are cooked, most of them deteriorate rapidly when held in the warming table, especially if the table temperature exceeds 150 degrees. Tender, quick-cooking vegetables should therefore be prepared as close to serving time as possible. If they must be cooked in advance, they should be slightly undercooked and allowed to reach completion in the serving trays. Trial and error will establish a workable time table. Vegetables which demand prolonged cooking can often be partially precooked and then brought to full tenderness immediately before serving time. Steamers minimize the problem, since almost any vegetable can be brought quickly to a done state this way, especially if the steam is pressurized.

Cooking times and conditions for fresh vegetables are given in Table 29 and for frozen vegetables in Table 30. Following the tables are several recipes offering comparative methods of cooking a variety of vegetables.

Table 29.
Timetable for Cooking Fresh Vegetables in Nonpressure Steamers*

Vegetable	Cooking Time (minutes)
Artichokes (medium size)	12
Asparagus	10
Beans, lima	12
Beans, string	20
Beets (according to size)	40-60
Broccoli (cut lengthwise)	15
Brussel sprouts	12
Cabbage (cut in sections)	12
Carrots (sliced)	15
Cauliflower (cut into flowers)	15
Celery (stalks)	15
Onions (small or quartered)	15
Peas	10
Turnips (medium size)	30

*   Times suggested in this chart will bring vegetables to a slightly under-done degree if they are cooked in shallow steam table pans or are otherwise not heaped thickly. Vegetables should always be thoroughly washed, cleaned, and trimmed; close leaf items such as Brussels sprouts, cabbage, cauliflower, and broccoli should also be soaked 15 minutes before cooking.

A pressure type steamer requires approximately 20 percent less cooking time.

Table 30.
Timetable for Cooking Frozen Vegetables

Vegetable	Cooking Time (minutes)		
	Boiled	Pressure Cooked	Steamed (no pressure)
Asparagus	15	1 ½	10
Beans, lima	20	3	12
Beans, string	16	4	18
Broccoli (flowers)	15	2	15

Table 30.
Timetable for Cooking Frozen Vegetables *(Continued)*

Vegetable	Cooking Time (minutes)		
	Boiled	Pressure* Cooked	Steamed (no pressure)
Brussel sprouts	12	1½	15
Corn (on the cob)	6	3	4
Corn (whole kernel)	6	1	12
Peas	8	1	15

*For pressure cooking add a small amount of water to the cooker and cook at 15 pounds pressure. All vegetables should be broken apart to facilitate cooking but need not be thawed.

Asparagus

	25 portions	100 portions
Fresh	10 lbs.	40 lbs.
Frozen	5 1-1b. cartons	2 cases (20 1-lb. cartons)
Canned	1 No. 10 can	4 No. 10 cans

Fresh Asparagus: Cut off tough ends (1 to 1½ inches from bottom). Tie in bunches of 12 or 15 stalks. Stand in hot water, tips up, allowing water to reach midway up stalk. Cover tightly, bring to a boil and reduce heat. Cook covered at a simmer for 20 minutes to *al dente* (slightly below the very tender stage).

In free venting, nonpressure type steamers, stand stalks in a small amount of water and steam for 10 minutes.

Frozen Asparagus: Empty cartons into cooking utensils, including any liquids frozen with the vegetables. Do not thaw. Add 2 cups of boiling water for each 5 lbs., cover and bring to a boil. Reduce and cook cut stems and tips for 6 minutes at a simmer while covered. For full spears cook covered at a simmer for 10 minutes.

Canned Asparagus: Simmer cut stems and tips together with surrounding juices for 6 minutes, whole spears for 10 minutes.

Suggested sauces: Cream sauce, hollandaise, or melted butter with salt and pepper.

Portion size: 2½ ounces asparagus and 1½ ounces sauce.

Green Beans

	25 portions	*100 portions*
Fresh	5 lbs.	20 lbs.
Frozen	5 1-lb. cartons	6 40-oz. cartons
Canned	1 No. 10 can	4 No. 10 cans

Fresh Green Beans: Remove tips and strings and cut into pieces. Add 2 inches salted water and any desired seasonings such as chopped onions, bacon fat, or chicken fat. Add beans and bring water to a boil. Reduce heat, cover well and simmer for 30 to 40 minutes or until tender. Chicken or beef stock may be substituted for water. In free venting, nonpressure type cookers, cook in 2 inch layers with a small amount of water. Sprinkle tops lightly with salt to prevent loss of color. Steam for 18 to 20 minutes.

Frozen Green Beans: Do not thaw. Put beans in cooking utensil with 1 cup of boiling water for each 25 portions and bring water again to a boil. Cook at a simmer for 15 to 20 minutes until tender.

Canned Green Beans: Using the surrounding liquids in the can, bring to a boil, reduce fire, cover, and cook at a simmer for 10 minutes.

Suggested flavoring enhancers: Butter or oleomargarine, bacon, salt pork, sweet and sour sauce, chopped onions, chopped parsley or tomatoes.

Portion size: 3 ounces with surrounding sauce or liquid.

Lima Beans

	25 portions	*100 portions*
Fresh (shelled)	4 lbs.	16 lbs.
Frozen	4 1-lb. cartons	6 40-oz. cartons
Canned	1 No. 10 can	4 No. 10 cans

Fresh Lima Beans: Cover with liquid and seasonings. Bring to a boil. Reduce heat to a simmer for 20 to 30 minutes or until tender.

To steam in free venting, nonpressure type cookers, cook in 2 inch layers with a small amount of hot water for 12 to 15 minutes. A pinch of baking soda added to the cooking water will preserve the bright green color, otherwise diminished in steaming.

Frozen Lima Beans: Do not thaw. Cover with very hot or boiling water, reducing to a simmer when the thawing has taken place. Cook for 10 to 12 minutes or until tender.

Canned Lima Beans: Using surrounding liquids, if any, add enough water to cover and bring to a boil. Reduce heat to a simmer for 10 to 15 minutes or until tender.

Suggested flavoring enhancers: Ham stock, ham shanks, bacon bits and pieces, bacon fat, chicken stock, chopped onions, shallots, or butter.

Suggested sauces: Cream sauce, tomato sauce, butter, or oleomargarine.

Portion size: 2½ ounces of beans and 2 ounces sauce or liquids.

Beets

	25 portions	*100 portions*
Fresh	5 lbs.	20 lbs.
Canned	1 No. 10 can	4 No. 10 cans

Fresh Beets: Cut off tops, leaving ½ inch. Leave roots attached. Wash in cold water. Cover with salted water and bring to a boil. Reduce heat and simmer for 1 hour for small young beets or 1½ hours for large older beets. Allow to cool in the cooking water. Rub off skins with the hands, pinch off tails and tops.

Canned Beets: Canned beets are ready to use and need only warming or combining with sauces to complete a recipe.

Suggested flavoring enhancers: Melted butter, sugar, or sweet and sour sauce for Harvard beets.

Portion size: 3 ounces.

Broccoli

	25 portions	*100 portions*
Fresh (stalks)	7 lbs.	28 lbs.
Frozen (stalks)	5 1-lb. cartons	2 10-lb. cases
Frozen (cuts)	4 1-lb. cartons	1 10-lb case plus 6 1-lb. cartons

Fresh Broccoli: Remove any outside leaves and tough parts of stalks (about 1 inch from the bottom). Stand with heads up in sufficient hot water to reach the bottom part of the heads. Bring water to a boil. Reduce heat to a simmer, cover well and cook for 20 minutes or until stems are *al dente* (partly done). Allow to remain in hot water, covered, for another 10 minutes.

In free venting, nonpressure type cookers, fill pans 2 layers deep, add ½ inch warm water and cook for 15 minutes.

Frozen Broccoli Stalks: Do not thaw. Stand stalks in 1 inch warm water. Bring water to a boil, reduce heat, cover well and cook at a simmer for 20 minutes.

Frozen Broccoli (cut stalks and heads): Do not thaw. Put in a pot, add 1 inch of water and bring to a boil. Cover well. Reduce heat and simmer for 15 minutes.

Suggested sauces: Hollandaise sauce, lemon butter, cream sauce or cheese sauce.

Portion size: Fresh or frozen stalks, 3 ounces. Frozen cut stalks and heads, 2½ ounces.

Carrots

	25 portions	*100 portions*
Fresh (peeled)	5 lbs.	20 lbs.
Frozen (sliced or quartered)	5 1-lb. cartons	2 10-lb. bags
Canned (sliced)	1 No. 10 can	4 No. 10 cans

Fresh Carrots: Cover with water and bring to a boil. Reduce fire and cover. Cook at a simmer for 20 minutes or until tender. Sliced or quartered, cook for 15 minutes.

Frozen Carrots: Do not thaw. Place in pot with small amount of warm water. Bring to a boil, then reduce fire to cook for 15 minutes or until completely thawed and hot.

Canned Carrots: Same method as for frozen.

Suggested flavoring enhancers: Cream sauce, bacon bits and pieces fried crisp together with drippings, sugar, butter sauce, or chopped parsley.

Portion size: 3 ounces.

Corn

	25 portions	*100 portions*
Frozen (whole kernel)	5 1-lb. cartons	2 10-lb. begs
Canned (whole kernel)	1 No. 10 can	4 No. 10 cans
Canned (creamed style)	1 No. 10 can	4 No. 10 cans

Frozen Corn: Do not thaw. Place in pot with a small amount of water. Bring water to a boil, reduce fire and cover. Cook at a simmer for 10 minutes.

Canned Corn: Heat and serve.

Suggested flavoring enhancers: Butter or oleomargarine.

Portion size: 3 ounces.

Green Peas

	25 portions	*100 portions*
Frozen	5 1-lb. cartons	2 10-lb. bags
Canned	1 No. 10 can	4 No. 10 cans

Frozen Peas: Do not thaw. Cover with boiling water and bring to a boil. After thawing is completed, reduce heat and simmer for 6 minutes.

Canned Peas: Heat and serve.

Suggested flavoring enhancers: Butter or oleomargarine, sugar, crisp fried bacon ends and pieces together with drippings, cream sauce, or finely chopped parsley.

Portion size: 3 ounces.

Spinach

	25 portions	*100 portions*
Fresh	9 lbs.	36 lbs.
Frozen	1 10-lb. bag	4 10-lb. bags
Canned	1 No. 10 can	4 No. 10 cans

Fresh Spinach: Wash spinach thoroughly in several waters. Allow final rinse water to cling to the leaves. Place leaves in pot with a small amount of water (approximately ½ inch). Bring water to a boil. Cover and reduce to a simmer for 10 minutes.

In free venting, nonpressure type cookers place spinach to a depth of 3 or 4 inches in pans. Add no water. Steam for 6 minutes.

Frozen Spinach: Thaw until spinach can be broken into fist-size pieces. Cover with very hot water and bring to a boil, cooking for 10 to 15 minutes or less if the large, still frozen pieces thaw and begin to cook. Actual cooking time should be 6 minutes after complete thawing.

Canned Spinach: Heat and serve.

Suggested flavoring enhancers: Salt, fresh ground pepper, butter or oleomargarine, bacon fried crisp together with drippings, or chopped hard boiled eggs.

Portion size: 3 ounces.

26.

Poultry

Either creamed and combined with other foods or served sliced, chicken and turkey offer a fine low-cost meat ingredient for extended dishes. Fried chicken is also an economical nutritious and popular entree. For dicing or slicing, poultry may be cooked by moist methods or slow-roasted. Moist heat cooking, while it does not produce a crust, does yield more cooked meat per pound of body weight.

To steam either chicken or turkey, place the birds in a shallow pan, allowing them to reach room temperature before they are placed in the steamer. Steam chickens 10 minutes per pound in free venting type steamers of the nonpressure type, or 8 minutes per pound in a pressure cooker set at 15 pounds pressure. Begin the timing when full pressure has been reached. Steam turkeys for 12 minutes per pound, or 9½ minutes per pound in pressure cookers set at 15 pounds pressure. This latter method is limited to birds of 12 pounds or less. To simmer, place the birds in boiling water and allow the liquid to return to the boiling point. Reduce and cook at a simmer at a point just below boiling. Cook both turkeys and chicken 20 minutes per pound. (When a number of chickens are cooked together use an average body weight.) For shrinkage control, let the birds then cool in the cooking liquid.

Roast chicken or turkey should be cooked on their sides rather than with breasts up. This will prevent the breast juices from draining when the cooking is finished. Birds require turning during the cooking process so that each side will cook evenly. Slow roasting at 350 degrees will require 25 minutes per pound for chickens and 30 minutes per pound for turkeys.

Because of their low meat yield to body weight, ducks are generally uneconomical for institutional use, although they are sometimes prescribed for dietetic purposes in hospitals or convalescent units. Low temperature roasting yields the best results. Cook at 350 degrees, allowing 20 minutes per pound of body weight for ducklings and 25 minutes for mature fowls.

For frying chicken in quantities suitable for institutional purposes, the following recipes for dredging flour and cooking will be of practical use.

Dredging Flour

(sufficient for 50 pounds of meat, fish, or poultry)

Hard wheat flour (bread flour)	2 lbs.
Potato flour	1 lb.
Salt	6 oz.
Dry milk solids	4 tbsp.
White pepper	1 tsp.
Paprika	3 tbsp.
Monosodium glutamate	4 tbsp.

Method: Mix all ingredients until thoroughly blended. Allow 1 ounce of seasoned flour for each pound of meat or fowl for light breading, more proportionately for heavier breading.

This flour may be kept indefinitely outside of refrigeration.

Home Style Pan-Fried Chicken

Chicken cut to serving portions
Dredging flour (see recipe above)
Frying fat
1 tbsp. water (approximately) for each lb. of chicken

Method: Dredge chicken with heavy coating of flour mix. Heat ½ inch layer of cooking fat or oil in a large skillet or a multiple of skillets for quantities. Fat should be very hot (about 350 degrees) before frying. Place chicken in the skillet, browning the fleshy pieces first by placing them skin side down in the skillet. Less meaty pieces can then be placed between the larger pieces as the cooking proceeds. Do not crowd the skillet. When browned well on one side, turn pieces and brown on the second side, using tongs to prevent piercing and moisture loss. When the chicken has been evenly browned (approximately 10 minutes) reduce the heat, add water, cover tightly and cook slowly for 40 to 45 minutes or until well done and tender. Uncover and cook rapidly at high heat for several minutes on each side to crisp the coating.

Remove from the skillet and keep in a warming table until ready to serve. At a temperature of 150 degrees chicken will hold an hour to an hour and a half without continuing to cook or fragmenting.

Pre-fry and Bake-off
Oven Fried Chicken

Chicken, cut up or halves
Dredging flour (see recipe)
Melted butter or oleomargarine
Chicken broth

Method: Dredge chicken thoroughly. Brown quickly (about 5 minutes) in a deep fat fryer with cooking fat at approximately 350 degrees. Place browned pieces in shallow oven pans, one layer deep. Spoon mixture of equal parts of melted mutter and chicken broth over the chicken, allowing about 1 ounce per pound of chicken. Finish cooking in 375 degree oven for 35 to 40 minutes. If the chicken appears to become dry while cooking, baste with a small amount of the butter and broth mixture. Remove to warming table when finished.

Rather than baking immediately after browning, the chicken, in oven pans, can be held uncooked under refrigeration. This advance preparation avoids excessive holding time in a warming table and also allows for meal preparation during slack periods in the kitchen.

Chicken prepared by this oven fried method is recommended for serving large groups either at once or over a relatively limited period. The product will hold its crispness well in a warming table maintained at approximately 150 degrees.

27.

Sauces and Gravies

Sauces and gravies play an important part in all institutional cooking procedures. They add taste appeal, portion volume, and nutritional benefits obtainable in no other way. As a continuation of the meat portion of the entree, they extend the volume of food that will comprise the total serving quantity. The nutritional and taste enhancements are derived from the food elements in the sauce or gravy, most springing from the juices of meats with added flavorings and starches.

For general purposes, sauces fall into two categories: white sauces which have chicken stock for a base and the brown variety which have meat juices such as beef, veal, lamb, or pork as a base. Both are versatile. The white sauce (or Bechamel) lends itself to seafood dishes, creamed dishes of all kinds, and as an underlay for fried entrees such as cutlets or chicken fried steaks. Brown sauce (or Sauce Espagnole) is used with many meat servings and vegetables or can be the base for many special subsauces. These two basic sauces will suffice as standards for the type of programs outlined in this book. Recipes for both sauces follow.

Brown Sauce (Espagnole)

	2 quarts	*2 gallons*
Onions, chopped fine	½ lb.	2 lbs.
Celery, chopped fine	4 ozs.	1 lb.
Green pepper, chopped fine	½ lb.	2 lbs.
Garlic, cloves, crushed	1	3
Mushrooms, sliced	4 ozs.	1 lb.

Brown Sauce (Espagnole) *(Continued)*

	2 quarts	2 gallons
Beef stock	1 qt.	1 gal.
Tomatoes, stewed	3 cups	1 No. 10 can
Tomato sauce	1 cup	1 No. 5 can
Sugar	1 tbsp.	4 tbsp.
Salt	1 tbsp.	4 tbsp.
Ground black pepper	½ tsp.	2 tsp.
Paprika	2 tbsp.	8 tbsp.
Monosodium glutamate	1 tbsp.	4 tbsp.
Cooking fat	½ cup	1 lb.
Flour	½ cup	2 cups

Method: Cook onions, celery, green pepper, garlic, and mushrooms in enough beef stock to cover ingredients, simmering until vegetables are slightly soft. Add balance of beef stock, stewed tomatoes, tomato sauce, sugar, salt, pepper, paprika, and MSG and cook at a simmer for 1 hour. Melt cooking fat and stir in flour and simmer for 5 minutes. Add cooked flour to the sauce and simmer for 10 minutes until the sauce is smooth and thickened.

White Sauce (Bechamel)

	2 quarts	2 gallons
Chicken stock	2 qts.	2 gals.
Parsley, sprigs	2	8
Bay leaf, small	¼	1
Onions, chopped	½ cup	2 cups
Carrots, chopped	½ cup	2 cups
Celery, chopped	½ cup	2 cups
Peppercorns, crushed	4	16
Hot milk	1 qt.	1 gal.
Salt	1 tsp.	4 tsp.
Butter	1 cup	2 lbs.
Flour	1 cup	1 qt.

Method: Simmer chicken stock with parsley, bay leaf, onions, carrots, celery, and peppercorns until reduced by half its volume. Strain and add hot milk and salt to remaining liquid. Bring to a simmer. Melt butter and add flour, cooking for 5 minutes. Add to sauce and continue to simmer for 10 minutes or until sauce is smooth and thick.

28.

Soups

Soups play an important part in institutional cooking. The commercial restaurant uses soup either as a leader to complete a meal service or as a low-cost a la carte menu item. Hospitals depend upon soup for dietetic purposes where light feeding is required. Directors of school feeding units supplying hot lunches mandate its use as an energy building food supplying a large percentage of daily vitamin and protein needs. In rest homes for the aged or in convalescent units soup is a convenient light meal and a source of vital nutritional energy. Detention units often use enriched soups for midday feeding for persons in inactive confinement and as a source of energy food for those on work details where its use is augmented with additional bulk foods.

As noted in the earlier discussion of kitchen equipment, where large quantities of soup are prepared and considerable amounts of fortified stocks are necessary, large stationary cooking kettles are vital for efficient production. For portion projections and for estimating the cooking capacities needed in the preparation kitchen, a safe guide is 6 gallons of soup to approximately 100 portions of 1 cup each, which is a normal serving.

All soups have a relatively low food cost, since most kitchens have sufficient by-products for making stocks which would otherwise become waste. Food produced through trimming, such as meat bits and pieces, bones or fats, tomato parts, green tops of some root vegetables, onion parts, or potato ends and pieces, can be used for producing a high grade stock, with each added item increasing the food value of the liquid. The liquids resulting from simmered meats and poultry become a prime ingredient which, when fortified by vegetable components, need only the addition of bulk material to create a high quality, extremely nutritious soup.

For convenience in serving and preparation, most large units prefer to use thin soups which are no more than rich stocks fortified with other ingredients. Creamed soups are more difficult to prepare in quantity and more difficult to handle in the warming table since they will often "break" if retained under heat for a prolonged period. Furthermore, most of them can not be successfully reheated. Creamed soups also have a higher degree of contamination potential if retained below 150 degrees in the warming table or above 50 degrees under refrigeration.

Small units whose production is less than several gallons will find success in using commercially prepared soup bases. These institutional types of bases are effective flavoring agents, as are the stocks, and their extra cost is often outweighed by their convenience. The nutritional values of such bases are equal and sometimes superior to those of stocks, making them especially useful in small hospitals, rest homes, or convalescent units. Such bases require an adjustment in house recipes since all commercial bases contain both salt and monosodium glutamate. Clear consommes, often a requirement in diet-oriented institutions, can be quickly produced from such bases.

Vegetable Soup

	25 portions (1½ gallons)	100 portions (6 gallons)
Beef stock	1 gal.	4 gals.
Parsley, chopped fine	4 tbsp.	1 cup
Tomatoes, canned	1 No. 2½ can	1 No. 10 can
Barley	5 tbsp.	1¼ cups
Bay leaf, crumpled	1 small	2 medium
Carrots, diced	1 lb.	4 lbs.
Celery, cut in chunks	8 ozs.	2 lbs.
Onions, diced	8 ozs.	2 lbs.
Rice, uncooked	4 tbsp.	1 cup
Potatoes, diced	1 lb.	4 lbs.
Green peppers, diced	½ cup	2 cups
Corn, canned, whole kernel	1 No. 2½ can	1 No. 10 can

Vegetable Soup *(Continued)*

	25 portions (1½ gallons)	100 portions (6 gallons)
Salt	2 tsp.	8 tsp.
Ground black pepper	½ tsp.	2 tsp.
Monosodium glutamate	2 tsp.	8 tsp.
Tabasco sauce	dash	1 tsp.

Method: Combine all ingredients and bring to a boil. Reduce fire and cook at a simmer for 1 hour.

Jellied Consommé

(Yield: 1 gallon)

Unflavored gelatin	3 oz.
Prepared chicken soup base	6 oz.
Boiling water	1 gal.

Method: Combine gelatin and soup base. Gradually add the mixture to the boiling water, continuing to stir until the soup base and gelatin are thoroughly dissolved. Remove from heat and allow to cool. Refrigerate until jelled. Skim off any fats before serving.

Beef consommé may be made in the same manner by using prepared beef soup base in place of chicken.

Chicken Noodle Soup

	25 portions (1½ gallons)	100 portions (6 gallons)
Chicken stock	1 gal.	5 gal.
Onions, chopped fine	8 oz.	2 lbs.
Celery, chopped small	8 oz.	2 lbs.
Salt	1 oz.	4 oz.
Ground black pepper	1 tsp.	4 tsp.
Monosodium glutamate	1 tbsp.	4 tbsp.
Wide flat noodles, uncooked	8 oz.	2 lbs.
Rice, uncooked	8 oz.	2 lbs.

Method: Bring stock to a boil and add onions, celery, salt, pepper, and MSG. Reduce to a simmer for 10 minutes. Add noodles and rice and continue cooking for 25 minutes or until noodles are tender and the rice puffy.

29.

Salads

Salad preparation and service often poses a problem where large numbers are to be served in a short period. To avoid delays, planning is vital. The simple mixed green salad with dressing is surprisingly the most difficult to contend with if it is served at its peak of perfection. Greens should be washed and crisped before serving. Crisping can be done two ways: chop the greens to the proper size and store them in plastic bags in a refrigerator up to 8 to 12 hours; or chop the greens and put them into a large stock pot, filling it 2/3 full and covering with very cold water. They may then be refrigerated for 8 to 12 hours. The greens will increase in volume as they crisp, eventually expanding to fill the pot. With a walk-in type of refrigerator, a large amount of salad can be prepared this way. The greens should be well drained just before use. The crispness will be retained in the refrigerator for several hours after the draining. This process not only improves the taste and texture of the greens but increases the volume sufficiently to effect an economy. Crisped greens should be portioned on cold plates and held refrigerated on trays until serving time. The dressing should be added as near the serving time as practical; otherwise the greens will become soggy and limp.

To enrich simple green salads, proteins in the form of chopped meats, seafoods, eggs, peas, beans, or garbanzos can be mixed with the salads after crisping or used as toppings. Dressings can be enriched by the addition of dry nonfat milk solids to cream type dressings and either pure olive oil or poly unsaturated oil to vinegar and oil type dressings.

Premixed and premolded salads, either simple or enriched, are the least troublesome, for they can be prepared during slack times and held until service with the least possible chance of deterioration.

Portion yields for green salads are in Table 31.

Table 31.
Green Salad Quantities

Lettuce type	25 portions*	100 portions*
Iceberg	4	16
Romaine	3	18
Endive	1	4

*The average portion size is 5 ounces.

Macaroni Salad

	25 portions	50 portions
Macaroni, uncooked	1 lb.	2 lbs.
Water for cooking	as required	as required
Green onions, chopped fine	4	8
Green pepper, chopped fine	1 cup	2 cups
Sweet pickles, chopped fine	2 cups	4 cups
Pimiento, chopped small	1 tbsp.	2 tbsp.
Celery, chopped fine	1 cup	2 cups
Cheddar cheese, grated	8 oz.	1 lb.
Mayonnaise	1 qt.	2 qts.
Salt	1 tsp.	2 tsp.
White pepper	½ tsp.	1 tsp.
Dry mustard	½ cup	1 cup

Method: Cook macaroni in boiling salted water until tender (about 18 minutes). Drain and rinse in cold water. Combine macaroni with remaining ingredients and chill well before serving.

Molded Vegetable Salad

	25 portions	100 portions
Unflavored gelatin	1 oz.	4 oz.
Cold water	1 pt.	2 qts.
Boiling water	1 qt.	1 gal.
Carrots, cooked, diced	8 oz.	2 lbs.
Peas, cooked	8 oz.	2 lbs.
Green beans, cooked	8 oz.	2 lbs.
Beets, cooked	8 oz.	2 lbs.
Cabbage, shredded fine	4 oz.	1 lb.
Celery, chopped fine	1 cup	4 cups
White vinegar	½ cup	2 cups
Sugar	3 oz.	12 oz.
Salt	1 tbsp.	4 tbsp.
Monosodium glutamate	1 tsp.	4 tsp.

Method: Soak gelatin in cold water for 10 minutes. Pour into boiling water and dissolve. Allow to cool to room temperature. Combine gelatin with remaining ingredients and pour into flat pans and refrigerate until jelled.

Service: Three ounces for each portion.

Tomato Aspic

	25 portions	50 portions
Tomato juice	3 qts.	6 qts.
Sugar	¼ cup	½ cup
Salt	1 tbsp.	2 tbsp.
Onions, chopped small	½ cup	1 cup
Celery tops or pieces	2 cups	4 cups
Bay leaf, small, crumpled	½	1
Peppercorns	½ tbsp.	1 tbsp.
Unflavored gelatin	½ cup	1 cup
Tomato juice	1 pt.	1 qt.
Lemon juice	½ cup	1 cup

Method: Combine tomato juice, sugar, salt, onions, celery, bay leaf, and peppercorns and bring to a boil. Reduce heat, cover and simmer for 20 minutes. Soak gelatin in remaining tomato juice for 15 minutes. Strain hot tomato juice mixture and add gelatin mixture, stirring well to dissolve the gelatin. Add lemon juice. Chill until firm (about 4 hours).

Service: Cut in portion size squares and top with mayonnaise or place on a bed of creamed cottage cheese.

Cooked Salad Dressing

	1 quart	*1 gallon*
Eggs	6	24
Processed powdered potatoes	3 tbsp.	6 oz.
Sugar	6 tbsp.	12 oz.
Salt	1 tsp.	4 tsp.
Dry mustard	1 tbsp.	4 tbsp.
White pepper	½ tsp.	2 tsp.
Monosodium glutamate	1 tsp.	4 tsp.
Vinegar	1 cup	4 cups
Water	1½ cups	6 cups

Method: Beat eggs together in the top of a double boiler. Add potato powder, sugar, salt, mustard, pepper, and MSG. Mix together well with a wire whisk. Combine vinegar and water and add slowly to the egg mixture while keeping smooth with the whisk. Cook over hot water until thick and smooth, whipping occasionally while cooking. Cool and keep in refrigerator until needed.

Creamy French Dressing

	2 gallons
Catsup or chili sauce	1 No. 10 can
Mayonnaise	3 qts.
Sugar	1 cup
Garlic, cloves, crushed	1
Worcestershire sauce	1 tbsp.
Dry mustard	1 tbsp.
Salt	1 tsp.

Method: Combine all ingredients and mix well. Store in refrigerator except during service, when it should still be kept cool. Prolonged exposure to room temperatures will cause an ingredient separation.

Thousand Island Dressing

	1 gallon	2 gallons
Mayonnaise	2 qts.	1 gal.
Catsup or chili sauce	1 pt.	1 qt.
Cheddar cheese, grated	8 oz.	1 lb.
Eggs, hard boiled, chopped	4	8
Sweet pickles, chopped	1 pt.	1 qt.
Ripe olives, pitted and sliced	1 cup	2 cups
Green pepper, chopped fine	1 cup	2 cups
Green onions, chopped fine	½ cup	1 cup
Salt	1 tsp.	2 tsp.

Method: Combine all ingredients and mix well. Refrigerate.

30.

Desserts

In the restaurant or cafeteria, desserts are most frequently used as low cost, profit generating extras which are sold a la carte. In rest homes for the aged, desserts, along with a beverage, are sometimes used as a complete light meal. In convalescent units where light foods are often mandated by dietitians, desserts can form an important entree. In these latter situations the dessert should be enriched sufficiently to reflect the required food elements. Detention organizations typically use desserts both as part of at least one meal a day and as a between-meal sustenance for persons on work detail.

Almost all desserts can be classified as energy foods, for they rank high on the nutrient scale. In line with the Type A School Feeding Program maxim that foods must be made attractive to assure their consumption, desserts can easily be given an appealing look. Obviously, if a dish is both nutritious and attractive it will have a high degree of added value either in a restaurant, where choice is often based on appearance or in an organization, where eating sometimes must be encouraged. The enrichment of desserts is a relatively simple procedure. Either cream, butter, or dry milk solids are often the only additive ingredients necessary to give it the food elements required by dietetic standards. Many desserts can be prepared by ordinary recipes with only a creamed topping, sauce, or a globule of whipped cream needed for added enrichment.

The recipes given here are adaptable to various levels of use and are illustrative of those best suited to volume preparation.

Fig Bread Pudding

	25 portions	100 portions
Fresh figs	1 qt.	4 qts.
Bread, broken or cubed	3 qts.	12 qts.
Orange rind, grated	2 tbsp.	¾ cup
Eggs	4	16
Sugar	½ pt.	1 qt.
Salt	1 tsp.	2 tbsp.
Milk	2 qts.	2 gal.
Nutmeg	as needed	as needed

Method: Cover figs with boiling water and let rest for 15 minutes. Drain and cool. Remove stems from figs and chop coarsely. Place bread in greased baking pans. Sprinkle with grated orange rind. Scatter the figs over the bread evenly. Mix eggs, sugar, salt and milk. Pour over bread and figs. Sprinkle with nutmeg. Bake in 325 degree oven for 45 minutes or until firm.

Apple Pie Filling

	5 9-inch pies	15 9-inch pies
Apples	1 No. 10 can	3 No. 10 cans
Juice from apples (add water to make)	1½ pts.	2½ qts.
Cornstarch	3 oz.	9 oz.
Sugar	1¾ lbs.	5¼ lbs.
Cinnamon	2 tsp.	6 tsp.
Nutmeg	1 tsp.	3 tsp.
Ground cloves	¼ tsp.	1 tsp.
Lemon juice	2 oz.	6 oz.

Method: Bake in double pie shell for 45 minutes or until browned in 425 degree oven.

Enriched Pumpkin Pie Filling

                                    9 9-inch pies

Sugar	1 qt.
Salt	1½ tsp.
Cinnamon	1 tbsp.
Ginger	1 tbsp.
Ground cloves	1 tsp.
Mace	1 tsp.
Dry milk solids	2½ cups
Eggs, well beaten	1 qt.
Pumpkin	2½ qts. (3 No. 2½ cans)
Melted butter or oleomargarine	1 cup
Hot water	3 qts.

Method: Combine sugar, salt, cinnamon, ginger, cloves, mace, and dry milk solids and mix well. Add the eggs and pumpkin and mix well. Add butter to hot water and gradually stir into the pumpkin mix, whipping smooth with a wire whisk. Fill unbaked pie shells three-quarters full of pumpkin mixture. Bake at 425 degrees for 12 minutes to bake crust. Lower temperature to 325 degrees and finish baking (about 30 minutes) until the pumpkin custard is well set, checking to assure that the center of the pie is also set.

Stewed Prunes

	25 portions	*100 portions*
Prunes	5 lbs.	20 lbs.
Water	1 gal.	4 gal.
Sugar	2 lbs.	8 lbs.
Lemons, cut into thin slices	2	8
Oranges, cut into thin slices	1	4
Cinnamon	1 tsp.	4 tsp.
Whole cloves	4	16

Method: Combine all ingredients and cook at a simmer for 1 hour.

Enriched Spanish Cream

	25 portions	100 portions
Unflavored gelatin	4 tbsp.	16 tbsp.
Milk	1 cup	1 qt.
Salt	2 tsp.	2 tbsp.
Milk	2 qts.	2 gal.
Dry milk solids	1 cup	4 cups
Sugar	1 lb.	4 lbs.
Eggs, separated	12	48
Vanilla	1 tbsp.	4 tbsp.

Method: Dissolve gelatin in first amount of milk. Add salt. Scald second quantity of milk and add dry milk solids. Combine the two mixes. Stir sugar in well. Beat egg yolks well and add. Cook in a double boiler until thick. Beat egg whites with vanilla until stiff and fold in. Pour into 5-ounce custard dishes and chill well.

For additional enrichment serve with whipped cream topping.

Enriched Vanilla Cream Pudding
(Blanc Mange)

	25 portions	100 portions
Sugar	1½ lbs.	6 lbs.
Salt	1 tsp.	4 tsp.
Milk	2½ qts.	2½ gal.
Dry milk solids	1 cup	4 cups
Butter or oleomargarine	2 oz.	8 oz.
Eggs	8	32
Milk	1 cup	4 cups
Cornstarch	4 oz.	1 lb.
Vanilla	1 oz.	4 oz.

Method: Combine sugar, salt, milk, dry milk solids, and butter and heat over low fire. Beat eggs and add. Combine milk and cornstarch and add. Cook in a double boiler until thick (about 30 minutes). Add vanilla. Pour into 5-ounce custard cups and chill.

31.

Baking

Baking is strictly a matter of correct temperatures, measures, and weights—with little room for experimentation. Temperatures especially play an important part in the correct working of yeast doughs. Doughs will be hampered by any change in temperature at any stage of preparation.

Yeast is a single-celled organism requiring definite conditions of temperature, food, and moisture for its growth. The temperature conducive to the multiplication of yeast cells and the consequent leavening of the dough in which it is used is between 70 and 90 degrees, a range which is considered to be room temperature. Yeast is inactive below 40 degrees and will be destroyed by heat in excess of 132 degrees. In the 70 to 90 degree range yeast grows rapidly. This growth is the basis for fermentation which causes the dough to rise. During the rising process any distinct change in temperature where the dough is working will drastically affect its progress. A blast of chilled air will retard the working of a dough being either fermented or proofed; while a surge of warm air will cause the rising to accelerate. Such changes can alter the quality of the dough, making it porous and tough and causing it to rise unevenly while being baked. The ideal situation for proofing is an even, controlled temperature. For small batches of dough an unlighted oven with a pilot light will serve.

Basic doughs can be flexible enough to provide for various purposes. Bread doughs will serve equally well for rolls; basic sweet dough can be used for sweet rolls, breakfast rolls, coffee cakes, cinnamon rolls, etc. Most institutional kitchens can function adequately with only these two doughs, changing the forms and shapes of the products to meet requirements. The forms in Figures 25 and 26 are basic bread varieties.

After basic yeast doughs have been mixed they are fermented, or allowed to rise to double their bulk. At the ideal sustained temperature of 80 degrees this requires from 1½ to 2 hours. After the dough is properly fermented it is punched down to remove the accumulated gas, then made into the desired forms. The formed products are then allowed to proof until again raised to double their size. They are then ready for baking.

Dough may be retarded for later use through refrigeration. When the doughs have been mixed and fermented they are punched down and immediately placed in the refrigerator. Portions of the dough may be removed and used as needed, so that one large batch may be used over an extended period. The length of dough retardation depends on temperature. Between 34 and 38 degrees retardation will be effective from 24 to 36 hours. Between 39 and 42 degrees the holding time will diminish to between 12 and 14 hours, and at 43 to 50 degrees the holding time will fall to a maximum of 10 hours. The dough may also be frozen and held from 3 to 6 days without deterioration. Beyond that period, doughs tend to deteriorate on a graduated scale. Frozen doughs should be revived in a refrigerator, which allows them to return gradually to a higher temperature. Usually a mass of dough will return to a workable consistency in 6 to 8 hours.

Pie dough can be made in quantity and kept for several weeks by refrigerating at temperatures of approximately 38 degrees. Frozen, they will keep for prolonged periods. The doughs should be covered well with either waxed paper or a damp cloth for refrigeration or in freezer wrap for freezing. Pie shells can be formed in advance and either refrigerated or frozen. Refrigerated shells should be used within a week to 10 days, past which time they tend to become sticky unless individually wrapped. Frozen shells keep indefinitely and do not need thawing before being filled and baked.

Baking powder doughs are best used immediately after mixing. Biscuits can be partially cooked until fully raised and then held in the refrigerator or freezer and used as brown-and-serve products. Batters are a form of baking powder dough. They have a short use span unless properly refrigerated. If refrigerated they keep relatively well for 3 or 4 days. Unleavened baking powder doughs do not lend themselves to freezing.

1 = Long pumpernickel. 2 = Italian bread. 3 = American rye. 4 = Pullman loaf. 5 = Round cinnamon loaf. 6 = Braided loaf. 7 = French loaf. 8 = Jewish Challah. 9 = Six-strand braided loaf. 10 = Vienna loaf. 11 = Round pumpernickel. 12 = White Mountain bread. 13 = White pan bread.

Fig. 25. *Varieties of bread.*

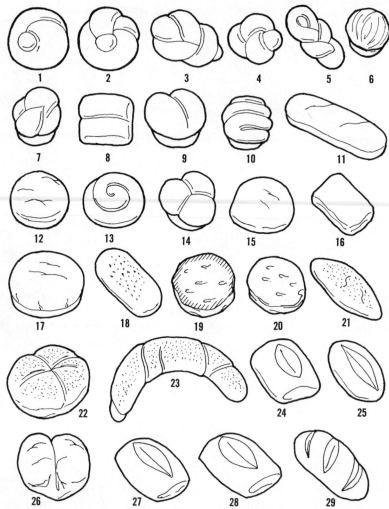

Soft rolls: 1 = Single knot. 2 = Double knot. 3 = Figure eight. 4 = Square knot. 5 = Braided roll. 6 = Spiral butter roll. 7 = Butter twist. 8 = Parker house roll. 9 = Twin roll. 10 = Butter roll. 11 = Frankfurter roll. 12 = Whole wheat roll. 13 = Spiral roll. 14 = Clover leaf roll. 15 = Pan roll. 16 = Snowflake roll. 17 = Hamburger roll. 18 = Poppyseed roll. 19 = Maryland roll with flour top. 20 = Vienna roll without flour top. 21 = Vienna bridge roll. **Hard rolls:** 22 = Kaiser roll. 23 = Crescent roll. 24 = French roll. 25 = Rye roll. 26 = Water roll. 27 = Small French roll. 28 = Club roll. 29 = Rye roll.

Fig. 26. *Varieties of rolls.*

Basic Bread Dough Mix

	30 pound mix	60 pound mix
Sugar	5 oz.	10 oz.
Warm water	1 qt.	2 qts.
Yeast	5 oz.	10 oz.
Milk	6 pts.	6 qts.
Sugar	1 lb.	2 lbs.
Salt	2 oz.	4 oz.
Warm water	5 pts.	5 qts.
Flour, hard wheat	15 lbs.	30 lbs.
Shortening	12 oz.	1½ lbs.

Method: Dissolve sugar in warm water. Crumble in yeast and allow to rest for 15 minutes. Scald milk and add sugar and salt to it. Allow milk to cool to lukewarm. Add warm water. Combine yeast mixture with water and milk. Add half the flour and mix well. Melt shortening and add. Add balance of flour. Knead lightly until well mixed and sticky. Turn into well greased pan or bowl, cover with damp cloth and set aside to ferment until doubled in volume. Punch dough down. It is now ready to use or store.

The 30-pound mix will yield approximately 25 loaves of bread or 125 rolls. The 60-pound mix will double these amounts. The large quantities are given here since most organizations prefer to mix doughs in advance of their needs and store them.

Pie Dough

(Yield: twenty-four shells or twelve double crust pies)

Flour	5 lbs., 8 oz.
Pure lard	4 lbs., 6 oz.
Salt	2½ oz.
Sugar	2½ oz.
Flour	1 lb., 2 oz.
Very cold water	1 qt.

Method: Mix together flour and lard until lard is in small, pea-size lumps. Mix the salt, sugar, flour, and water until smooth and add to the first mixture. Mix to a smooth dough. Keep under refrigeration until needed. This dough will remain in good condition for several days if covered with a damp cloth.

Basic Sweet Dough Mix

	14 pound mix	28 pound mix
Sugar	6 oz.	12 oz.
Warm water	1 pt.	1 qt.
Yeast	4 oz.	8 oz.
Milk	1 qt.	2 qts.
Shortening	14 oz.	28 oz.
Sugar	1 lb.	2 lbs.
Salt	4 tsp.	8 tsp.
Eggs, large	12	24
Flour, all purpose	7 lbs.	14 lbs.
Warm water	1 pt.	1 qt.

Method: Dissolve sugar in warm water. Crumble yeast and add. Mix and allow to rest for 15 minutes. Scald milk and add shortening to it. Cool to lukewarm. Add sugar and salt, dissolving well. Beat eggs and add to sugar mix. Add half of flour and yeast mix, combining well. Add water and the balance of the flour, mixing well. Knead lightly until the dough is rubbery. Place dough in a well greased bowl. Cover with light cloth and allow to ferment until double in size (about 2 hours in a 75 to 80 degree temperature). Punch down and allow to rest for 10 minutes. The dough is then ready to use or to store in refrigeration.

Waffle and Hot Cake Batter

	50 hot cakes or 25 waffles	200 hot cakes or 100 waffles
Flour	2 qts.	8 qts.
Baking powder	8 tsp.	4½ oz.
Salt	2 tsp.	1½ oz.
Sugar	4 oz.	1 lb.
Softened butter or oleomargarine	½ lb.	2 lbs.
Milk	2½ pts.	5 qts.

Method: Combine all ingredients in the order given and beat into a smooth batter. More milk may be added to thin the batter slightly for thinner hot cakes and crisper waffles. Use 2 ounces of mixture for hot cakes and 4 ounces for waffles. Keep under refrigeration.

Prepared Blend for Biscuit Flour

(Yield: 12 quarts)

Flour	10 lbs.
Baking powder	1 cup
Salt	6 tbsp.
Shortening	7½ cups

Method: Sift flour, baking powder, and salt into a large pan. Lift and stir with pastry blender to mix thoroughly. Cut in shortening with a pastry blender, mixing until the mixture resembles coarse meal. Store in a cool, dry place in loosely fitting covered cans. The product will keep in good condition for 8 to 10 weeks without refrigeration.

Biscuits from Blend

(Yield: 48 biscuits)

Prepared blend	3 qts.
Milk	3 cups

Method: Mix blend and milk into a soft dough and roll out on well-floured board to a thickness of ½ inch. Cut biscuits with 2-inch cutter. Bake in 425 degree oven for 14 to 16 minutes or until well browned.

32.

Volume Preparation Methods for Twenty-Five Low-Cost Entrees

The production recipes given here are for foods which fit conveniently into the portioning system outlined in the first section of the book. The amounts can be changed but are generally suitable for commercial restaurants and cafeterias. Just as the serving quantities can be altered, so can seasonings—either robust for general purposes or bland for use in hospitals and rest homes.

The meat cookery information in the first chapter of this section will be helpful in using these and similar formulas to arrive at a finished product with the proper texture, degree of doneness, and appearance. No matter how much other care goes into compounding a formula, undercooking will make the food inedible and overcooking will cause extreme shrinkage and an unappealing appearance.

The extenders in a volume formula comprise the bulk of the meal in most cases. Therefore, care should be taken to assure that vegetables are added in correct sequence and, just as in the case of meats, cooked to the right degree—palatable yet not fragmented from too much cooking or from wrong temperatures. This also applies to noodles, rice, macaroni, or, for that matter, any other food that has a decided peak of cooking perfection. Sauces or surrounding gravies should neither be over thick nor thin and watery. In a volume feeding operation offering low-cost entrees and dealing with inexpensive foods, care in preparation and service is the most vital ingredient.

Simple principles support these twenty-five illustrative, low-cost production formulas. First, they must be created from low-cost meats or utilize leftovers or by-products resulting from trimming other primal cuts. Second, their essential economy lies in the use of filler material to form their bulk. Meats used in dishes of this type should never equal the amount of filler material; rather, it should in most cases amount to less than one-third of the gross bulk. In meatless formulas, expensive additions such as eggs, olives, mushrooms, etc., should take the same lower ratio, serving primarily as seasoning ingredients or garnishes.

Formulas of this type are highly flexible. Braises of all kinds, for example, may be served alternately with either noodles or rice, making it unnecessary to include a potato in any form. If such a dish is not intended for a single-item entree, a green vegetable can serve as an auxiliary food item and a garnish. Creamed dishes can take either a potato, rice, or noodles to fill out the plate. Meat loaves or fish cakes can be extended with a gravy or sauce to enlarge the appearance of the portion as well as add food value to the plate. For other variations, steamed rice can be alternated with variously seasoned rice pilaff; and boiled noodles may be replaced with the crisp fried oriental type.

Baked Creamed Hamburger

	25 portions	*100 portions*
Melted butter or oleomargarine	¼ lb.	1 lb.
Ground beef	8 lbs.	32 lbs.
Salt pork, ground fine	½ lb.	2 lbs.
Bread crumbs	1 qt.	1 gal.
Onion, chopped fine	1 cup	4 cups
Black pepper	1 tsp.	2 tbsp.
Salt	2 tsp.	4 tbsp.
Monosodium glutamate	2 tbsp.	8 tbsp.
Milk	1 pt.	2 qts.
Cream sauce, warm	1 qt.	1 gal.

Method: Combine all ingredients except the cream sauce and mix very well. Shape into walnut-size balls and brown slightly by placing in baking pans in one layer and cooking in a hot (425 degree) oven for 15 to 20 minutes. Cover meat balls with cream sauce and continue baking in a 350 degree oven for 1½ hours.

Service: Three meat balls and a spoon of sauce on a bed of mashed potatoes, steamed rice, or cooked noodles.

Chicken a la King (Creamed Chicken)

	25 portions	50 portions
Chicken stock	2 qts.	1 gal.
Flour	8 oz.	1 lb.
Chicken fat or melted butter	8 oz.	1 lb.
Milk	1 pt.	1 qt.
Cooking oil	4 oz.	8 oz.
Fresh mushrooms, sliced	8 oz.	1 lb.
Onions, chopped fine	½ cup	1 cup
Green peppers, chopped small	1 cup	2 cups
Cooked chicken meat, cubed	3 lbs.	6 lbs.
Pimientos, chopped small	1 cup	2 cups
Salt	2 tsp.	2 tbsp.
Monosodium glutamate	1 tbsp.	2 tbsp.

Method: Heat chicken stock to a simmer. Make a paste from the flour and fat or melted butter and stir into the stock and simmer until thickened. Add milk and again bring to a simmer. Heat the cooking oil in a skillet and sauté the mushrooms, onions, and green peppers together until the vegetables are done. Add this mixture to the white sauce together with the cubed chicken meat, pimientos, salt and MSG and simmer the combined mixture for 10 minutes.

Service: Six ounces of the chicken mix can be served on toast points, over steamed rice, on a bed of noodles or encasserole with an accompanying portion of potatoes. The portions can be easily adjusted to fit any control program.

Creamed Tuna on Rice

	50 portions
Canned tuna (include juice)	4 lbs.
Eggs, hard-boiled, chopped coarse	12
Pimiento, chopped small	½ cup
Cooked green pepper, chopped small	½ cup
White pepper	½ tsp.
Monosodium glutamate	1 tbsp.
Cream sauce	4 qts.
Cooked rice	9 qts.

Method: Combine all ingredients except rice and bring to a simmer, cooking for 10 minutes to blend seasonings. Slight salting may be necessary if the cream sauce is bland.

Service: Four ounces of the tuna mix on a 4-ounce bed of hot, steamed rice. As an alternative, serve the mix on toast with a green vegetable or add fresh or frozen green peas to the mixture, in which case no additional vegetable is needed.

Ham and Egg Cutlet

	24 portions	*48 portions*
Smoked picnic or pork shoulder butt, cooked and boned	1 qt.	2 qts.
Eggs, hard boiled	18	36
Onions, quartered	1 cup	2 cups
Parsley, chopped fine	2 tbsp.	4 tbsp.
Butter or oleomargarine	½ lb.	1 lb.
Flour	1¼ cups	2½ cups
Milk	1 qt.	2 qts.
Salt	1 tbsp.	2 tbsp.
Monosodium glutamate	1 tbsp.	2 tbsp.
Cracker crumbs	1 pt.	1 qt.
Paprika	as required	as required
Cracker meal, fine	as required	as required

Method: Put meat, boiled eggs, onions, and parsley through a food grinder and mix well. Melt butter and combine with flour to form a smooth paste, adding milk gradually. Simmer until smooth and thick. Combine the two mixtures and add salt, MSG and cracker crumbs. Mix well. Press mixture into a pan 12 x 18 inches for 24 portions or two pans for the double lot and chill until quite firm (2 or 3 hours). Cut into equal portions when firm and dip individual cutlets into cracker meal and sprinkle with paprika. The cutlets can be oven-fried, pan-fried, or deep-fried. They should be cooked until well browned and crusted.

Service: Serve each cutlet with an underlining of cream sauce or for a single plate entree serve on toast points topped with cream sauce with either chopped boiled eggs or green peas.

Braised Fresh Beef Tongue

	10 portions
Beef tongue	5-6 lbs.
Onions, chopped fine	1 cup
Celery, chopped fine	1 cup
Carrots, sliced or diced	2 cups
Clarified butter or oleomargarine	½ cup
Flour	¾ cup
Water (or stock from tongue)	5 cups
Worcestershire sauce	2 tbsp.
Salt	1 tsp.
Ground black pepper	1 tsp.
Monosodium glutamate	1 tbsp.

Method: Cover the tongue with boiling water and simmer for 2 hours. Remove the skin and trim. Place tongue in casserole with the onions, celery, and carrots. Prepare a sauce by blending the flour and butter and adding to the stock or water and simmering until thickened. Season sauce with Worcestershire, salt, pepper, and MSG and pour over the tongue. Cover well and bake in 350 degree oven for 2 hours or until tongue is tender.

Service: Slice tongue. Serve two slices topped with a small amount of sauce.

Beef Dumplings

	25 portions	*50 portions*
Bread crumbs	6 cups	12 cups
Ground beef	6 lbs.	12 lbs.
Ground sage	2 tsp.	4 tsp.
Parsley, chopped very fine	1 cup	2 cups
Salt	2 tsp.	4 tsp.
Monosodium glutamate	2 tbsp.	4 tbsp.
Black pepper	2 tsp.	4 tsp.

Method: Soak bread crumbs in water and press dry. Combine all ingredients and mix into a smooth paste. Form into balls slightly smaller than an egg. Cook in simmering water for 1 hour, keeping each piece separated by stirring occasionally.

Service: Three pieces of dumpling. They may be served on a bed of cooked noodles, steamed rice, or mashed potatoes and topped with brown gravy, or they may be served with vegetables as a meat entree.

Ham and Lima Beans

	25 portions	100 portions
Salt pork, diced small	½ lb.	2 lbs.
Onions, chopped small	1 lb.	4 lbs.
Cooked lima beans	6 lbs.	24 lbs.
	(2½ lbs. raw)	(10 lbs. raw)
Salt	2 tsp.	4 tbsp.
White pepper	½ tsp.	2 tsp.
Cream sauce	1 qt.	4 qts.
Cooked smoked picnic or pork shoulder butt, diced into small cubes	4 lbs.	16 lbs.
Monosodium glutamate	1 tbsp.	4 tbsp.

Method: Brown salt pork well and add onions, continuing to cook until onions are tender. Combine all ingredients and heat to a simmer. Cook for 15 minutes.

Service: For a single plate entree serve 8 ounces.

Ham and Noodles au Gratin

	25 portions	100 portions
Cooked smoked picnic or pork shoulder butt, diced small	4 lbs.	16 lbs.
Cream sauce, thick	2 qts.	2 gal.
Cooked wide noodles	6 lbs.	24 lbs.
	(2 lbs. raw)	(8 lbs. raw)
Cheddar cheese, grated	1 lb.	4 lbs.
Paprika	as required	as required

Method: Combine smoked pork, cream sauce, and noodles, mixing evenly. Place in baking pans and sprinkle with grated cheese and paprika. Bake 30 minutes in 350 degree oven or until well heated and the cheese topping is melted.

Service: For a single plate luncheon serve 8 ounces per portion. Alternate methods of preparation: Use cooked macaroni in the same proportion as cooked noodles to make Ham and Macaroni au Gratin. For either Ham and Macaroni or Noodles with Spanish Sauce prepare as above by replacing the cream sauce with Spanish sauce.

Creamed Chipped Beef

	25 portions	50 portions
Dry chipped beef	1¾ lbs.	3½ lbs.
Butter or oleomargarine	4 oz.	8 oz.
Flour	2 cups	4 cups
Butter or oleomargarine	1 lb.	2 lbs.
Milk	1 gal.	2 gal.

Method: Sauté chipped beef in the first quantity of butter until heated through and starting to crisp. Combine flour and second quantity of butter and simmer together until well mixed and creamed but not browned (approximately 5 minutes). Heat the milk and combine with the flour and butter mixture and simmer until the sauce is thick and smooth. Add chipped beef.

Service: 6 ounces per portion. Creamed chipped beef is a flexible entree especially adaptable to luncheon programs of all kinds. The above mixture can be varied by serving it on toast points, over steamed rice or cooked noodles. For light luncheons or hot plate luncheon programs, the amount should be half that above, or approximately 3 ounces.

For dietary enrichment, add 2 tablespoons of dried milk solids to the smaller recipe or 4 tablespoons for the larger.

Breaded Veal Cutlets

	25 portions	100 portions
Eggs	3	12
Water	1½ cups	1½ qts.
Salt	1 tbsp.	4 tbsp.
White pepper	½ tsp.	2 tsp.
Monosodium glutamate	1 tbsp.	4 tbsp.
Flour	1½ cups	1½ qts.
Bread crumbs	1 lb.	4 lbs.
Veal cutlets, 3-oz. slices	25	100

Method: Combine the eggs and water. Combine salt, white pepper, MSG, flour, and bread crumbs. Dip the cutlets first into the egg mixture and then into the bread crumbs, pressing the crumbs in well. Cook in a skillet or on a grill until well browned on both sides. Cutlets may be cooked in advance and held in the warming table until served.

Service: Place cutlets on a bed of cream sauce and add potatoes or a vegetable. For a single plate entree they can be served on toast points topped with cream sauce and chopped or sliced hard cooked eggs. They may also be served on a bed of cooked noodles or steamed rice and topped with cream sauce.

For dietary enrichment, add 1 tablespoon of dry milk solids to each cup of flour in the breading process.

Cutlets may be cut from boneless veal leg or shoulder or purchased frozen in premolded and preportioned sizes.

Veal Fricassee

	25 portions 1 ½ gallons)	100 portions (6 gallons)
Boneless veal shoulder	5 lbs.	20 lbs.
Cooking fat or oil	½ cup	2 cups
Salt	2 tsp.	8 tsp.
Pepper	½ tsp.	2 tsp.
Carrots, sliced thin	1 lb.	4 lbs.
Celery, chopped coarse	½ lb.	2 lbs.
Onions, chopped coarse	1 lb.	4 lbs.
Parsley, chopped fine	1 tsp.	4 tsp.
Pimiento, chopped small	½ cup	2 cups
Bay leaf, small, crumpled to bits	½	2
Beef stock	3 qts.	3 gal.
Flour	1 cup	1 lb.
Butter or oleomargarine	1 cup	1 lb.
Peas, canned	1 No. 2½ can	1 No. 10 can

Method: Cut meat into 1-inch cubes and brown lightly in melted cooking fat or oil. Add salt and pepper and continue braising the meat for 30 minutes at a low temperature. Add carrots, celery, onions, parsley, pimiento, bay leaf and beef stock. Simmer after bringing to a boil for 1½ hours or until the meat is tender. Cream flour and butter together and cook over a low heat for 5 minutes, being careful not to brown. Add to fricassee and cook for 10 minutes longer until the gravy is thick. Stir in canned peas just before placing on serving table.

This recipe is very adaptable for use in various portioning programs. It can be served over beds of cooked noodles, in rice rings or in potato rings for single-plate dishes, or in casseroles with a fresh green vegetable. It meets many dietary standards for hot lunch programs and can be predished or served cafeteria style.

Shepherd's Pie

	25 portions	*50 portions*
Cooked beef, cubed	3½ lbs.	7 lbs.
Cooked green peas	1½ qts.	3 qts.
Cooked carrots, diced or sliced	1½ qts.	3 qts.
Cooked whole small onions	1½ qts.	3 qts.
Brown sauce or meat gravy	2 qts.	4 qts.
Whipped potatoes, well-seasoned	3 qts.	6 qts.

Method: Combine meat and vegetables in baking pans. Heat brown sauce or gravy and pour over the meat. Make a topping with whipped potatoes. Bake in 425 degree oven until slightly browned.

Service: Six ounces as a single item luncheon plate.

Oven-Fried Fish Fillets (Haddock, Sole, Halibut, or Any Boneless Fillets)

	48 portions
Fish fillets	12 lbs.
Salt	2 tbsp.
Milk	3 cups
Fine, dry bread or cracker crumbs	3 qts.
Melted butter or oleomargarine	2 lbs.
Paprika	as required

Method: Cut fillets into 4-ounce portions. Combine salt and milk. Dip fish pieces in milk and then into bread crumbs, repeating the process to double-coat fish with bread or cracker crumbs. Place fish in a baking pan that had been well greased with melted butter or oleomargarine and sprinkle with any remaining butter and paprika. Bake in 450 degree oven for 8 to 12 minutes according to thickness of the pieces or until they are well browned and crusted on all sides. Pieces may be tested with a fork for doneness. When well done the fish will flake easily.

Service: One piece per portion. As an alternate service for luncheon plates, cut the fillets to either 2- or 3-ounce portions and serve on a bed of cream sauce or tomato sauce. For a single plate luncheon entree serve smaller piece (2 or 3 ounces) on toast and top with cream sauce with added chopped hard boiled eggs or green peas.

Braised Oxtail Joints

	10 portions
Oxtails, cut into 2-inch sections	5
Onions, chopped fine	1 cup
Green pepper, chopped coarse	2 cups
Clarified butter or oleomargarine	½ cup
Flour	1½ cups
Salt	1 tsp.
Ground black pepper	1 tsp.
Stewed tomatoes, canned	4 cups
Ground ginger	1 tsp.
Beef stock	4 cups

Method: Cover cut pieces of oxtail with boiling water and allow to stand for 10 minutes and drain well. Sauté onions and green peppers in melted clarified butter until tender. Season flour with salt and pepper and dredge oxtail pieces well. Add meat to onions and peppers and brown lightly. Add tomatoes, ginger, and stock. Cover tightly and simmer for 2 hours or until meat falls away from the bones easily.

Service: Three or 4 pieces of oxtail topped with sauce.

Braised Sweetbreads

	6 portions
Sweetbreads, large	3 pairs
Salt pork	¼ lb.
Carrots, diced	2 cups
Celery, chopped coarse	1 cup
Parsley, chopped fine	1 tbsp.
Beef stock or water	1½ cups
Cream, light	½ cup
Sliced mushrooms, canned	1 cup

Method: Place sweetbreads in water, allowing them to stand for 1 hour, changing the water several times. Remove from water and blanch in salted boiling water for 15 minutes. Rinse in cold water. Remove tubes and membranes. Cut salt pork into larding strips and lard the sweetbreads. Place sweetbreads in casserole surrounded by carrots, celery, and parsley. Pour in stock. Cover and cook at a simmer for 1 hour. Remove sweetbreads from the casserole and place on serving tray. Force vegetables and remaining stock through a sieve. Add cream and mushrooms. Adjust seasoning and bring to a simmer. Pour sauce over sweetbread for serving.

Curried Lamb, East India Style

	25 portions	100 portions
Boneless lamb shoulder or breast cut into 1-inch cubes	8 lbs.	32 lbs.
Water	as required	as required
Milk	3 qts.	3 gal.
Flour	6 oz.	1½ lbs.
Melted butter or oleomargarine	¾ lb.	3 lbs.
Cooking oil	1 cup	4 cups
East Indian curry powder	3 tbsp.	12 tbsp.
Tabasco sauce	½ tsp.	2 tsp.
Monosodium glutamate	1 tbsp.	4 tbsp.
Onions, chopped fine	1 lb.	4 lbs.
Apples, cored but unpeeled and sliced thin	1 lb.	4 lbs.

Method: Cover lamb cubes with water and cook at a simmer for 1½ hours or until tender. Drain and reserve the cubes. Heat milk to a simmer and thicken with a paste made from the flour and melted butter, stirring long enough to make smooth and thick. Heat cooking oil in a pan large enough to hold the meat and vegetables. Blend the curry powder, tabasco sauce, and MSG into the oil and work into a smooth paste. Add cooked lamb meat, onions, and apples and stir together well, cooking at a simmer while covered for 30 minutes. Combine the meat sauce and the white sauce and mix well.

Service: For a single plate entree, 6½ ounces of curry mixture on a 4-ounce bed of steamed rice. For an attractive luncheon plate garnish the serving with a pineapple slice topped with 1 ounce of chutney.

Braised Beef Tips with Noodles

	25 portions	*100 portions*
Boneless beef	8 lbs.	32 lbs.
Salt	1 oz.	4 oz.
Black pepper	½ tsp.	2 tsp.
Flour	1 cup	4 cups
Paprika	1 tbsp.	4 tbsp.
Cooking oil	1 cup	4 cups
Green peppers, chopped coarse	2 lbs.	8 lbs.
Onions, chopped coarse	2 lbs.	4 lbs.
Beef stock	1 qt.	4 qts.
Tomato sauce or puree	2 cups	8 cups
Cooked noodles	6 lbs.	24 lbs.
	(2 lbs. raw)	(8 lbs. raw)

Method: Cut beef into 1-inch cubes. Sprinkle with salt, pepper, flour, and paprika and mix well. Place cooking fat in heavy oven pan and add meat cubes. Cook for 30 minutes in 350 degree oven. Remove from oven and add green peppers, onions, beef stock, and tomato sauce. Stir together well. Return to the oven and simmer for 1½ hours or until meat is tender.

Service: As a single plate entree serve 8 ounces meat and gravy over 6 ounces of cooked noodles. Variations in service: For other single entree plates serve the meat mixture over a bed of steamed rice or mashed potatoes.

Beefsteak and Kidney Pie

	25 portions	*50 portions*
Beef chuck meat	6 lbs.	12 lbs.
Beef kidney	4 lbs.	8 lbs.
Brown gravy flavoring	½ cup	1 cup
Cooking oil	1 cup	2 cups
Water or beef stock	1 qt.	2 qts.
Monosodium glutamate	1 tbsp.	2 tbsp.
Salt	4 tsp.	4 tbsp.
Black pepper	1 tsp.	1 tbsp.
Celery, chopped small	2 lbs.	4 lbs.
Onion, chopped fine	1½ lbs.	3 lbs.
Carrots, diced or sliced thin	1 lb.	2 lbs.

Method: Cut meat into 1-inch squares (removing tubes from kidneys). Stir in brown gravy seasoning to coat meat evenly. Heat cooking oil and brown meat slightly. Combine meat with water or beef stock and simmer for 1 hour. Add all other ingredients and continue cooking for 1 hour or until meat is tender. Place 6 ounces in casserole and top with pastry topping rolled thin. Bake in 425 degree oven until top is brown (about 20 minutes).

Tamale Pie

	25 portions	*50 portions*
Yellow corn meal	5 lbs.	10 lbs.
Water	4 cups	8 cups
Salt	1 tbsp.	2 tbsp.
Onions, chopped small	2 cups	4 cups
Green peppers, chopped coarse	2 cups	2 cups
Cooking oil	½ cup	1 cup
Ground beef	5 lbs.	10 lbs.
Tomatoes, canned	1 No. 10 can	2 No. 10 cans
Whole kernel corn, drained	1 No. 5 can	1 No. 10 can
Chili powder	2 tbsp.	4 tbsp.
Monosodium glutamate	1 tbsp.	2 tbsp.
Salt	2 tsp.	2 tbsp.

Method: Combine corn meal, water, and salt in top of double boiler. Cook 1 hour, stirring frequently. More water may be added to keep mush from becoming dry. Sauté onions and peppers in cooking oil until tender then add meat. Mix well and cook until done. Add tomatoes, corn, chili powder, MSG, and salt. Cook together until mixture is thick (about 15 minutes). Line greased baking pans with half the mush mixture, making the crust about 1 inch thick. Pour meat mixture evenly over the layer of mush. If more than one pan is used, divide meat mixture equally. Cover meat mixture with a crust of the remaining corn meal mush. Bake in 350 degree oven for 1 hour or until topping is slightly browned.

Service: As a single plate luncheon serve 3½-inch squares. For a mixed plate serve a 3-inch square and add an accompanying green vegetable.

Irish Stew (Lamb Stew)

	25 portions	*100 portions*
Boneless lamb shoulder or breast cut to 1-inch cubes	6 lbs.	24 lbs.
Water	4 qts.	4 gal.
Salt	2 tbsp.	8 tbsp.
Onions, chopped fine	1 cup	4 cups
Bay leaf, small, crumpled	1	4
Parsley, chopped fine	½ cup	2 cups
Flour	6 oz.	1½ lbs.
Water	1½ cups	6 cups
Potatoes, diced	2 lbs.	8 lbs.
Carrots, diced or sliced	2 lbs.	8 lbs.
Canned peas, drained	1 No. 5 can	2 No. 10 cans
Onions, quartered	1 lb.	4 lbs.
Monosodium glutamate	1 tbsp.	4 tbsp.
White pepper	½ tsp.	2 tsp.

Method: Cover meat cubes with the first quantity of water, add salt, onions, bay leaf, and parsley. Bring to a simmer and cook until the meat is tender, or approximately 1½ hours. Make a paste of the flour and the second quantity of water and add to the meat, cooking until the gravy thickens. Cook the vegetables in boiling water, adding the canned peas last just before removing from the heat. Drain the vegetables and add to the meat mixture. Stir in the MSG and white pepper and simmer the stew for 10 minutes to blend.

Service: Eight-ounce single plate entree.

Rice and Tuna Croquettes

	50 portions
Cooked rice	1¼ qts.
Canned tuna, water pack	2 lbs.
Eggs, separated	12
Onions, chopped fine	3 cups
White pepper	1 tsp.
Cayenne	¼ tsp.
Parsley, chopped	2 tbsp.
Lemon juice	2 tbsp.
Dry bread crumbs	1 qt.
Paprika	3 tsp.

Method: Combine cooked rice, tuna, egg yolks, onion, pepper, cayenne, chopped parsley, and lemon juice, mixing well until smooth. Chill for 1 hour. Stir in slightly beaten egg whites and form into croquettes weighing approximately 1½ ounces each. Roll croquettes in mixture of bread crumbs and paprika, coating well. Deep-fry or oven-fry until well browned and crusted.

Service: Two croquettes with cream sauce or tomato sauce. For a single entree luncheon plate serve two croquettes on toast points and cover with a cream sauce containing diced hard boiled eggs or green peas.

Escalloped Oysters

	50 portions
Oysters, small	1 gal.
Celery, chopped small	1 qt.
Melted butter or oleomargarine	1 cup
Flour	1½ cups
Salt	2½ tbsp.
White pepper	1 tsp.
Monosodium glutamate	2 tbsp.
Milk	3 qts.
Fresh bread cubes	2 gal.
Melted butter or oleomargarine	¼ cup
Dried bread crumbs	1 pt.

Method: Drain oysters and reserve the liquid. Simmer chopped celery in oyster liquid for 10 minutes. In a large saucepan combine butter, salt, pepper, MSG, and milk. Add flour. Cook over low heat until thick and smooth. Add celery and oyster liquid to sauce and simmer together for several minutes. Alternate layers of bread cubes, oysters, and cream sauce in two buttered pans approximately 12 x 20 inches x 2½ inches deep, ending with a layer of sauce on top. Combine melted butter and bread crumbs and sprinkle on top of each pan. (For taste and appearance this topping may be colored by adding paprika, grated Parmesan cheese, finely chopped parsley, or a combination of the three.) Bake in 425 degree oven for 30 minutes.

Service: Serve 4½ ounces on plate with green vegetable for luncheon plate or with vegetable and potato for a dinner plate.

Baked Meat Casserole

	25 portions	50 portions
Bacon, chopped in small pieces	½ lb.	1 lb.
Leftover cooked chicken, veal, or pork or a combination, cubed or diced	3 qts.	6 qts.
Flour	1 cup	2 cups
Carrots, sliced thin	1 qt.	2 qts.
Green pepper, diced small	1 qt.	2 qts.
Onions, chopped fine	1 qt.	2 qts.
Salt	1 tbsp.	2 tbsp.
Hot chicken or beef stock	2 qts.	1 gal.
Monosodium glutamate	1 tbsp.	2 tbsp.

Method: Fry bacon until crisp, drain off fat. Add diced meats and mix, heating thoroughly. Add flour and cook until the meats are well browned. Mix carrots, green pepper, onions, and salt. Combine hot stock with MSG. Cover the bottom of a baking pan with half the meat mixture. Place the vegetables over the meat. Make a topping with the remaining meat. Pour hot stock over the combined ingredients. Bake in 350 degree oven for 1½ hours or until vegetables are tender and well done.

Cabbage Leaves with Ham and Rice

	25 portions	50 portions
Onions, chopped fine	8 oz.	1 lb.
Cooking oil	4 tbsp.	½ cup
Cooked smoked picnic or pork shoulder butt, diced small	3 lbs.	6 lbs.
Ham or meat stock	1 pt.	1 qt.
Tomatoes, canned	1 pt.	1 qt.
Sugar	4 tsp.	8 tsp.
Cooked rice	2 qts.	1 gal.
Cabbage, large leafy heads	3	6
Water for cooking cabbage	as required	as required

Method: Cook onions in oil until tender. Add meat, stock, tomatoes, sugar, and rice and stir together. Remove from heat. Separate cabbage leaves, taking care to keep them whole and as large as possible, and parboil them 3 minutes. Roll approximately 3 ounces of the ham and rice mixture into each cabbage leaf and place side by side in a baking pan. Bake 20 minutes in 350 degree oven or until well heated.

Service: 2 rolls per portion. As an alternate service for a single plate luncheon, cover the cabbage rolls with tomato sauce while baking. Serve two rolls and 3 ounces of sauce for an entree. Another alternative is to sprinkle the rolls with bread crumbs and grated Parmesan cheese before baking and serve over 2 ounces of tomato sauce.

Braised Short Ribs of Beef

	24 portions	*48 portions*
Beef short ribs	18 lbs.	36 lbs.
Caramel food coloring	½ cup	1 cup
Cooking fat	¾ lb.	1½ lbs.
Onions, chopped small	2 pts.	2 qts.
Celery, chopped small	1 pt.	1 qt.
Green peppers, chopped coarse	1 lb.	2 lbs.
Salt	2 tbsp.	4 tbsp.
Ground black pepper	1 tbsp.	2 tbsp.
Powdered thyme	1 tbsp.	2 tbsp.
Water	1½ qts.	3 qts.
Flour	1 cup	2 cups
Water	1 cup	2 cups
Monosodium glutamate	1 tbsp.	2 tbsp.

Method: Cut short ribs into individual servings and coat with caramel coloring. Melt cooking fat and brown the meat in it until well seared and crisp on all sides. Add onions, celery, green pepper, salt, pepper, and thyme, cooking until vegetables are lightly browned. Add water. Bring to a boil, reduce to a simmer and cover tightly. Cook 1½ to 2 hours or until meat is tender. Remove cover and mix flour, water and MSG and add, continuing to cook until the gravy is thick (5 to 10 minutes).